HOMELESSNESS

HOMELESSNESS

WHOSE PROBLEM IS IT?
TED GOTTFRIED

Issue and Debate
The Millbrook Press
Brookfield, Connecticut

For Sara Reyes Brink and Caleb Rudolph Kornmann,
two welcome new arrivals—peace and love always.

Photographs courtesy of Impact Visuals: pp. 8 (© Clark Jones), 42 (©
Evan Johnson), 46 (© Andrew Lichtenstein), 53 (© Donna Binder), 56
(© Donna Binder), 64 (© Rick Reinhard), 76 (© Donna Binder), 99 (©
Harvey Finkle); The Image Works: pp. 13 (© Mitch Wojnarowicz), 79
(© Michael Siluk), 93 (© David H. Wells); North Wind Picture
Archives: pp. 18, 24; Children's Aid Society: p. 21; Corbis-Bettmann:
p. 27; Culver Pictures: p. 29; UPI/Corbis-Bettmann: pp. 31, 34

Library of Congress Cataloging-in-Publication Data
Gottfried, Ted.
Homelessness : whose problem is it? / Ted Gottfried.
p.   cm. — (Issue and debate)
Includes bibliographical references and index.
Summary: Discusses the issue of homelessness, examining who the
homeless are, how they become that way, and differing views on how to
deal with the problem.
ISBN 0-7613-0953-5 (lib. bdg.)
1. Homelessness—United States—Juvenile literature.
[1. Homelessness.] I. Title. II. Series.
HV4505.G68   1999
305.569—dc21   98-22484   CIP   AC

Published by The Millbrook Press, Inc.
2 Old New Milford Road
Brookfield, Connecticut 06804

CONTENTS

ACKNOWLEDGMENTS

I am indebted to my longtime friend Lee Kreiling, former Director of Scattered Site Housing for the New York Coalition for the Homeless, for her advice and vetting of the manuscript of this book. Rudy Kornmann, Anita Yulsman, R. D. H., Kathryn Paulsen, Tom Coakley, and my daughter Julie Coakley were very helpful in amassing the research.

The personnel of various branches of the New York Public Library were also helpful and courteous.

Thanks as always to my wife, Harriet Gottfried, for her understanding and patience. Such support was invaluable, but any errors, or shortcomings, are mine alone.

hough studies show conflicting information about numbers and makeup of the homeless population, ryone agrees that homelessness is a problem that st be addressed. This grouping of shelters built by homeless was photographed in New York City.

OPPOSING VIEWPOINTS

*"When I was seventeen I got pregnant, dropped
out of school, and moved in with my boyfriend.
After a few years I became so afraid of his beat-
ings that I took my two children and moved
out. I was all alone and unable to get a job. I
haven't seen my dad since he left my mother
when I was seven, so I can't turn to him for help
and my mom kicked me out when I had my first
baby. . . ."*

Anna, a homeless woman who was moved
with her children from shelter to shelter.[1]

Is Anna a victim or a weak-willed young woman who
brought her misfortune upon herself? Has she failed
to play by the rules and deliberately avoided work?
Does society have an obligation to rehabilitate Anna
and care for her children? Should she be rescued,
or should she have to live with the consequences
of her actions?

There are many young women like Anna among
the homeless in the United States. Like Anna, many

start out as unmarried teenagers with babies. Their circumstances vary, but they have one thing in common: They do not have permanent housing.

They are not alone. The homeless are not all teenage single mothers. Their ranks include men as well as women, old people as well as young, city people and country folk, the mentally ill and the physically impaired, drug addicts and alcoholics, immigrants and native-born Americans, war veterans and victims of domestic violence, members of all ethnic groups, races, and religions.

Nobody knows exactly how many people are in the different groups that make up the homeless population. Nor is it known how many homeless people there are altogether. Indeed, the debate about homelessness begins with the question of just how many people are homeless. Estimates vary widely. A 1994 U. S. Department of Housing and Urban Development study put the number of homeless Americans during the second half of the 1980s at between five and nine million people.[2] These are people who were without housing at some point during that period, but they were not necessarily all homeless at the same time. Some—perhaps many—of them may not be homeless any longer. Others who had homes at the time of the survey may be homeless today. A 1993 study by Dr. Bruce Link of Columbia University indicated that some twelve million adult Americans had been homeless at some point in their lives.[3]

Based on these and other surveys, advocates for the homeless estimate that the 1997 homeless population averaged a minimum of three million people. Critics say that figure is much exaggerated. They point to a 1990 survey of the homeless by the

U. S. Census Bureau, which put the total at only 230,000.

However, the Census Bureau itself admits that its 1990 survey is flawed and that "the data do not represent a complete count of the homeless population."[4] What the Bureau did was compile a list of people in shelters in 14,200 localities and then add to that number those street people that interviewers were able to locate on a single night—March 21, 1990. Those homeless who were out of sight that night were not counted, and because cities with populations under 50,000 weren't included, the homeless in small cities and rural areas were also bypassed.

Advocates for the homeless and their critics agree that an accurate count of the homeless population is difficult, if not impossible, to obtain. The population is constantly changing, with new people becoming homeless and homeless people finding housing. And while there is a steady core of people who remain homeless, there is wide disagreement as to their numbers.

CAUSES AND BLAME

Advocates for the homeless blame both government and business for the problem. They say federal, state, and local housing policies encourage the construction of middle-income and luxury dwellings, but don't create enough low-rent dwellings. "People become homeless because they can no longer afford housing" writes Joel Blau in his book *The Visible Poor: Homelessness in the United States.*[5] He blames recent homelessness on downsizing (companies firing workers) and the transfer of manufacturing jobs overseas where workers can be paid much lower wages than in the United States. Those who agree see job loss as causing depression, alcoholism, domestic violence, family breakups, and other problems that contribute to homelessness. And they also accuse society of perpetuating homelessness by failing to provide enough treatment programs for drug addicts, alcoholics, and the mentally ill.

On the other side, some see homelessness as part of the welfare dependency cycle that is passed on from one generation to the next. They view a breakdown in morality and family values as responsible for creating a population of homeless single teenage mothers who would rather rely on welfare than work. They regard most addicts and alcoholics as products of self-indulgence. The mentally ill street people, in their opinion, should not have been let out of institutions. People, they say, have an obligation to provide for their own old age and if they haven't, then their children and families, not the government, have a duty to care for them.

Lawrence Mead, professor of political science at New York University, blames homelessness on bad judgment. "If poor people behaved rationally," he says, "they would seldom be poor for long in the first place."[6] It follows that if they were not poor, they would not be homeless.

COMPASSION VS. "TOUGH LOVE"

There is also disagreement about how to approach the problem. Advocates claim that understanding, sympathy, and compassion must be the starting point. They believe in providing the necessities, such as food, clothing, shelter, and medical care on

The homeless are not confined just to large cities. This 1991 photograph shows Paul, a homeless man, in the small city of Amsterdam, in upstate New York. He claimed to have wandered all over the Northeast.

a regular basis as a first step. They believe that the problem is so great that only government can fund the programs necessary to deal with homelessness.

Critics of this approach feel that charity for the homeless should be a private matter, not a government obligation. They feel that the homeless must face reality and be responsible for themselves rather than relying on others. A "tough love" approach encompassing workfare and length-of-time restrictions on benefits is viewed as the way to end welfare dependence by the homeless. They also insist that any solution must include a realistic appraisal of how it impacts on the quality of life of the community at large.

Every solution has a downside in some people's eyes. Welfare increases dependency and prolongs homelessness. Workfare impacts on the labor market and turns the working poor into the jobless—and sometimes the homeless—poor. (These programs will be discussed later in the book.) Massive government aid for the homeless means additional taxes for the rest of us, including the working poor. Withdrawing such aid means that helpless, blameless children will go hungry. Providing housing for the homeless in stable neighborhoods creates fear among the families in those neighborhoods. But if this "Not In My Back Yard" (NIMBY) thinking determines policy, then the homeless are doomed to choose among overcrowded slums, unsafe shelters, and the streets.

The problem of homelessness is large and complicated. But it's not a new concern. Homelessness in America has been a major issue throughout its history.

2
NO ROOF
OVER THEIR HEADS

Homelessness is as old as the United States itself. When the first European settlers arrived on the shores of North America, they were homeless. They slept under the stars or put up crude lean-tos to protect themselves from the elements while they built more permanent dwellings. Hunters and trappers relied on animal hides and caves and hollowed-out riverbanks for shelter. Farm families huddled with their livestock under makeshift overhangs of burlap or grass and leaves.

As the country became more settled and cities sprang up, people built houses. Some of these were subdivided to offer rooms to travelers and sailors in port while their ships unloaded. Often the rooms contained as many as eight or ten beds. Sometimes beds were rented out by shares with two or even three or four lodgers occupying one berth for the night.

There were those, however, who couldn't even afford to share a bed. These people included the unemployed, the disabled, alcoholics, wives who had run away from abusive husbands, and children who had been forced to leave home because there was not enough money to feed them. There were also recent immigrants.

THE EARLY IMMIGRANT HOMELESS

The first cities were seaports, such as New York, Boston, and Philadelphia, and the largest number of temporarily homeless people in these ports were newly arrived immigrants. They had undergone incredible hardships to cross the Atlantic Ocean. In 1750, Gottlieb Mittelberger described one such voyage: "During the journey the ship is full of . . . smells, fumes, horrors, vomiting . . . sea sickness, fever, dysentery. . . boils, scurvy, cancer, mouth-rot and similar afflictions, all of them caused by the age . . . of the meat, as well as by the very bad and filthy water. . . ."[1]

Those who survived reached port in terrible shape. They were sick. Often they had lost their loved ones. Many children who had set out with their parents arrived as orphans. Many of the adults were unfit for work. These unfortunates became a large segment of the mounting population of homeless who slept under the docks and in shacks thrown up behind the shipping company warehouses.

In 1737 a letter in the *New York Journal* lamented the condition of homeless street urchins in the city. It spoke of a child who was "an Object in Human Shape, half starv'd with Cold, with Cloathes out at the Elbows, Knees through the Breeches, Hair standing on end. . . . From the age about four to Fourteen they spend their Days in the Streets. . . ."[2]

In the smaller towns of New England the homeless fared no better. "Newcomers" who wanted to settle in a town "were by definition homeless and often without resources, raising a concern whether they would mean additional tax burdens for the town. . . . Widows and children as well as disabled or aged adults were often 'warned' to leave town. There thus arose a kind of transient poor, shunted from community to community. . . ." [3]

After the American Revolution, the Articles of Confederation, the document that temporarily linked the thirteen colonies as a nation, denied the "privileges and immunities of free citizens" to "paupers, vagabonds, and fugitives from justice."[4]

When the United States Constitution replaced the Articles of Confederation, however, the denial of rights to paupers and vagabonds was dropped. Nevertheless, in many sections of the new country homeless "vagrants, transients, and 'strollers' . . . could be jailed, dumped in the workhouse, or sold [for labor]."[5]

THE CENTRAL PARK SQUATTERS

By the 1840s the homeless were migrating to the West, where land was plentiful and cheap—sometimes free. They staked out farms and planted crops and built houses. The people in the covered wagons had been migrant, and so temporarily homeless, but were homeless no more.

At the same time new immigrants were flocking to the port cities of the United States. Most of the newcomers were German and Irish. Many of them were unskilled and penniless and formed the core of a new homeless population.

This nineteenth-century etching shows squatters near what would one day become Central Park in New York City. It was a mostly undeveloped area on the outskirts of the city, and the poverty-stricken, many of them immigrants and former slaves, claimed it as theirs.

THE SQUATTERS OF NEW YORK—SCENE NEAR CENTRAL PARK.—[SKETCHED BY D. E. WYAND.]

In New York City they drifted to the wooded area that would one day become Central Park. Parts of this area had been purchased and settled by African Americans, some of them former slaves. The new immigrants who came there, however, were "squatters," people who did not own the land on which they lived. Egbert Viele, the park's first engineer, remembered it as "the refuge of about five thousand squatters, dwelling in rude huts of their own construction, and living off the refuse of the city." He described them as people "with very little respect for the law."[6] They were driven off between 1853 and 1857, when work on different areas of the park began, but over the years Central Park would often be a refuge for the homeless.

The Orphan Trains

Half a million people lived in New York City in 1850. Historians record that 30,000 homeless children were among them.[7] They slept in doorways and empty buildings and ate out of garbage pails or stole food. According to the law, seven-year-olds were adults and could go to jail for stealing. Children over twelve could be hanged in public.

Many of these children had run away from abuse in their homes, or from orphanages where conditions were dreadful. Because overcrowding was a real problem in these orphanages, runaways were not usually pursued.

In 1853, Charles Loring Brace, a New York minister, started the Children's Aid Society to help the street urchins. The following year, Reverend Brace initiated the first of the so-called orphan trains, which would carry homeless children from the big cities to farm country. The orphan trains ran sporadically between 1854 and 1930, carrying almost half a million homeless children to the West. The idea was that the children would find new homes and families there. Some did find good homes with foster parents. Some were treated as farmhands or servants, and fed and housed in exchange for their labor. More than a few of the children were beaten and mistreated in other ways.

THE UPROOTED OF THE CIVIL WAR

When the Civil War began in 1861, many homeless men joined the armies of both the Union and the Confederacy. The devastation of the war, however, created a new homeless population. Homes and crops were destroyed. Women and children, especially in the South, wandered the countryside trying to stay out of the way of hostile forces.

The South's slave population was uprooted by the war. Many young black men made their way north to join the Union army, where they served with distinction. Homeless families of former slaves journeyed to unsettled areas and built homes, planted crops, and established communities. But the majority, both during and after the war, found that the immediate result of freedom without resources was hunger, joblessness, and homelessness. Many ex-slave families were forced by such circumstances to go back to the plantations from which they had come to work for their former masters. They rarely owned their own homes, and during hard times over the years that followed they would be driven out of them.

After the Civil War, the homeless population continued to grow. By the 1870s opposing views of

Homes Wanted
For Children

A Company of Orphan Children

of different ages in charge of an agent will arrive at your town on date herein mentioned. The object of the coming of these children is to find homes in your midst, especially among farmers, where they may enjoy a happy and wholesome family life, where kind care, good example and moral training will fit them for a life of self-support and usefulness. They come under the auspices of the New York Children's Aid Society. They have been tested and found to be well-meaning boys and girls anxious for homes.

The conditions are that these children shall be properly clothed, treated as members of the family, given proper school advantages and remain in the family until they are eighteen years of age. At the expiration of the time specified it is hoped that arrangements can be made whereby they may be able to remain in the family indefinitely. The Society retains the right to remove a child at any time for just cause, and agrees to remove any found unsatisfactory after being notified.

Remember the time and place. All are invited. Come out and hear the address. Applications may be made to any one of the following well known citizens, who have agreed to act as local committee to aid the agent in securing homes.

A. J. Hammond, H. W. Parker, Geo. Baxter, J. F. Damon, J. P. Humes, H. N. Welch, J. A. Armstrong, F. L. Durgin.

This distribution of Children is by Consent of the State Board of Control, and will take place at the

G. A. R. Hall, Winnebago, Minn.

Friday, Jan. 11th, '07, at 10.30 a. m. @ 2 p. m.

Office: 10

This notice advertises "A company of orphan children," which would arrive in Winnebago, Minnesota on January 11, 1907. Between about 1854 and 1930, "orphan" trains carried nearly half a million homeless children to the West.

the homeless began to take shape. Professor Francis Wayland of Yale University presented one opinion at the 1877 Conference on State Charities. He defined a certain jobless man as "a person without a home who was unwilling to labor." He went on to paint a grim picture: "He will outrage an unprotected female or rob a defenseless child or burn an isolated barn . . . or wreck a railway train, or set fire to a railway bridge, or murder a cripple, or pilfer an umbrella . . . ."[8]

But a quite different description of the 1870s tramp is presented by Michael Katz in his study, *Poverty and Policy in American History.* They were not, writes Katz, "drunks or illiterates. Nor did they constitute a permanent class. . . . Most had a trade. They were circulating between cities, stopping most often in country towns, looking for work. . . . It is hard to imagine that most tramps were dangerous, a threat to the honor of women, [or] the security of property. . . ."[9]

These different views extended to homeless women and children. Heated debates arose over whether they should be given small amounts of money, provided with shelter in poorhouses, or ignored because "relief encouraged the lazy and immoral to look to the public treasury for support rather than to earn their living. . . ."[10] The question, still being argued today, was how to help the deserving poor without coddling the undeserving.

SKID ROWS AND POORHOUSES

During the 1870s, and extending into the twentieth century, the transient homeless were mostly able-bodied men. They were unskilled laborers and migrant workers who moved from place to place to pick the crops, or to work in the mines and factories. As often jobless as not, they drifted to the cities in cold weather.

Areas known as skid rows sprang up in many American cities. (The term "skid row" came from the popular slang expression "on the skids," used to describe a person sliding helplessly down into destitution.) Here a man could get a bed for the night for pennies. Many begged for those pennies and shared their night's lodging with bedbugs. In the cheap bars that flourished on skid rows, many blotted out their despair with rotgut whiskey bought with the other pennies they had panhandled.

The women on skid row were mostly prostitutes. Other homeless women—widows, deserted wives, unemployed and unmarried females, those who were old and sick—often ended up in poorhouses run by local governments. Conditions in the poorhouses were terrible. They were overcrowded, understaffed, and underfinanced. They tended to be filthy, lice-infested places whose residents received little health care and were fed small amounts of rancid foods.

Most poorhouse residents were elderly. Men outnumbered women by approximately two to one. An 1892 study by Mary Roberts Smith, professor of social science at Stanford University, pointed out that one reason this was so was that it was "a most disgraceful thing for relatives or children to allow an old woman to go to the almshouse." The 1910 Census Bureau found that homeless women, both young and old, were more likely than men to be "taken care of by relatives, friends, or even private charities."[11]

Conditions in nineteenth-century urban "flophouses" (dirty, cheap places where homeless men could pay for shelter for the night) were seldom better than those on the streets themselves.

Throughout the 1890s and 1900s concern mounted over the number of homeless children on the streets. In the wake of stock market crashes in 1901 and 1907, many factories were forced to close and tens of thousands of workers lost their jobs. There were many children among them.

The situation of these children in the 1900s is described in *Chronicle of the Twentieth Century*: "In the United States, more than 1.75 million children under 16 years old work in factories. . . . 200,000 of them are under 12. Six- and seven-year-old girls work 13 hours a day spinning cotton."[12] When their jobs disappeared, these children, like their elders in the mills and factories, often found themselves without money, food, or shelter.

Another spin-off effect of the loss of jobs was the desertion of wives and children by husbands no longer able to support them. In 1909, in Manhattan, 3,000 men abandoned their families, a 33 percent increase over the previous year. Most of the men were between the ages of twenty and twenty-four and left two or more children behind.

THE STOCK MARKET CRASH OF 1929

Homelessness nationwide was relieved in 1914 when war broke out in Europe. By 1917, when the United States entered World War I, factories manufacturing weapons and other supplies were running full-steam. As young men left for the army, older homeless men and some women and children took over their jobs. With the prosperity created by the war, homelessness declined. Soon only a small number of homeless were left—the most unemployable.

Prosperity continued into the 1920s. Congress passed laws limiting immigration, and this helped reduce the numbers of new homeless. On the other hand, labor turmoil in which unions were crushed and workers were locked out pushed some workers and their families into homelessness. Periodic crop failures throughout the decade added farm families to the ranks of those without shelter. Nevertheless, the 1920s saw a continuation of the trend of decreased homelessness in the United States begun during the war.

In October 1929, the trend was abruptly reversed with the crash of the stock market and the beginning of the Great Depression. "Between 1929 and the summer of 1933, official unemployment in America climbed from 3.2 percent to 24.9 percent," writes Michael B. Katz, professor of history at the University of Pennsylvania.[13] It was only a short step from joblessness to homelessness.

THE OKIES AND THE ARKIES

During the Depression, droughts in Arkansas and Oklahoma caused small farmers and sharecroppers to lose their land and their homes. Whole families packed up their belongings in old jalopies and flatbed trucks and headed west in response to handbills advertising jobs for farm laborers in California. By 1937 a congressional investigating committee would find that five million people (nicknamed "Okies" and "Arkies" after their home states) were on the road moving from state to state in search of jobs and housing. But there were countless thousands more on the move than there were jobs, and many of them

A group of Oklahomans stop on the road in New Mexico in this 1937 photo. The droughts in their state drove these now homeless "Okies" west to seek work and fertile land, which would prove difficult to find.

were turned back by state troopers at the California border.

John Steinbeck described what it was like in his novel of the Depression, *The Grapes of Wrath*: "And the dispossessed, the migrants, flowed into California, two hundred and fifty thousand and three hundred thousand. . . . [There were] golden oranges hanging on the trees . . . and guards with shotguns patrolling the lines so a man might not pick an orange for a thin child, oranges to be dumped if the price was low. . . . "[14]

THE BONUS MARCHERS

Among the homeless were many veterans of World War I. For serving in the war they had been given bonus certificates for money to be paid them years in the future. But they needed that money now to provide homes for their families.

In the spring of 1932, World War I veterans organized a march on Washington to petition Congress to give them their bonus money. Many of them had been living in makeshift communities of wooden shacks with tin roofs called "Hoovervilles," after President Herbert Hoover, whom many blamed for the Great Depression. Now they set up the largest Hooverville of all, a city of old wood and tarpaper and canvas housing 20,000 men, women, and children on the outskirts of Washington, D.C.

The bill to give them their money passed the House, but was defeated in the Senate. The veterans refused to leave, and President Hoover ordered the army to evict them. Commanded by General Douglas MacArthur (later to lead U. S. ground forces in the Pacific during World War II), four troops of

Many of the Great Depression-era homeless were veterans of World War I. In 1932 they joined other veterans in a massive march on Washington, D.C., to petition Congress to pay them the bonus money it had promised them for serving in the war.

cavalry, four companies of infantry, a machine-gun squadron, and six tanks moved on the veterans. Tear gas was used to clear them out. Their shelters were torched. When it was over there were three dead, including an eleven-week-old baby. A thousand veterans had been injured by the gas, and an eight-year-old boy had been blinded by it.

THE NEW DEAL

A few months later Herbert Hoover was swept out of office and Franklin Roosevelt was elected president. A New Deal to relieve Depression suffering was decreed. Bonus marchers were encouraged to return to Washington to renew their demands. President Roosevelt ordered that they should be given food and medical care. Eleanor Roosevelt, the president's wife, went to visit them and reported that they were "grand-looking boys with a fine spirit." One of the veterans noted that while "Hoover sent the Army, Roosevelt sent his wife."[15]

The New Deal swung into action with the Federal Emergency Relief Act to help the large population of migrants seeking work during the Depression. It was followed by the Works Progress Administration (WPA), which created new jobs for the unemployed, many of whom were homeless. Federal unemployment insurance was introduced. Social Security was established to protect people against the hardships of old age and the threat of homelessness.

Two New Deal programs, Aid for Dependent Children (ADC) and Aid to Families with Dependent Children (AFDC), marked the beginning of federal welfare programs. "The American welfare state

The programs of the New Deal alleviated some of the effects of unemployment, which helped to ease the homeless problem brought on by the Depression. These young men, working with the Civil Conservation Corps (CCC), were clearing burned areas in the state of Washington.

emerged in the 1930s divided between public assistance and social insurance," observes Professor Katz. "Public assistance has become synonymous with welfare; it carries the old stigma of relief."[16]

THE WAR YEARS

The New Deal programs helped, but there was still much suffering and homelessness during the Depression. Genuine improvement only came with the beginning of World War II in Europe in 1939. Factories reopened, and, as during World War I, production of war materials created jobs, which provided spending money for working people, which resulted in more manufacturing, more jobs, and more spending money. Throughout the war years of the 1940s, and beyond, the economy boomed, and homelessness didn't seem to be a major problem.

Fueled by fear of the Communist Soviet Union, the boom continued through the 1950s. There were still homeless people, but they were more or less the invisible poor confined to skid rows or the worst slum neighborhoods. No longer were there vast numbers of homeless families roaming the country in search of work as there had been during the Depression years.

While there were still many poor whites, particularly from Appalachia, among the 1950s homeless, there was also an increase in minorities. There was a migration of young black men, many of whom had served in the war, from the South to the North. They came seeking jobs in manufacturing, but even in boom times there was a limit to the number of such jobs, and inevitably some of these men ended up homeless in cities like Detroit and

Pittsburgh. There was also an influx of Americans from Puerto Rico seeking jobs in New York and other northern cities. Some of these people also became homeless.

HOMELESS ON PURPOSE

The 1960s saw a new kind of homelessness. Middle-class high school and college age youngsters voluntarily left their homes to become street people. Their opposition to the war in Vietnam caused them to distrust any form of "the Establishment." Some of them used drugs. This was not a homelessness of need, but of choice. Added to the skid row alcoholics, they formed a picture in the public mind of the undeserving poor who sponged off both government and private citizens.

Most of the 1960s homeless, however, were not alcoholics, drug addicts, or young rebels. They were the truly needy who lacked skills and jobs and a place to lay their heads. The War on Poverty programs of President Lyndon Johnson were aimed at them. Programs like Operation Head Start introduced prekindergarten instruction to break the cycle of poverty passed down from parent to child. Job training programs were set up for adults. Slum clearance eliminated skid rows.

Many skid row slum-clearance programs backfired. The idea had been to eliminate slums where the housing was old, dilapidated, and crumbling. But the government made no provisions for replacing the skid rows. In many cases developers stepped in and put up housing that poor people could not afford. The homeless were deprived of the skid row flophouses and moved on to other neighborhoods.

— 33

A new type of homeless person in the 1960s was one who wished to show distrust for "the Establishment" by dropping out of society. Doing just that, these young people occupied an abandoned farmhouse in Pennsylvania in 1968.

With their departure, the support services on which they had depended were no longer needed. Missions that provided free clothing, second-hand stores, pawn shops, and soup kitchens disappeared. The former skid row area was no longer attractive nor hospitable to the homeless.

In 1963 the Community Mental Health Center Act resulted in the release from institutions of those mentally ill people who were not dangerous. They were to live either in group homes or in single-room occupancy (SRO) dwellings, and they were to continue receiving treatment as outpatients.

But people didn't want group homes for the mentally ill in their neighborhoods, and landlords wanted to convert SROs into more profitable rental units. Too often finding themselves deprived of shelter, many of the mentally ill couldn't cope with getting their medications on schedule from the outpatient clinics. By the 1970s more and more of them were wandering the streets, sleeping in hallways, parks, and bus terminals.

The 1970s saw the beginning of the modern era of homelessness. The most noticeable change was that the homeless became much more visible. One reason for this was the shortage of low-cost housing for the poor in cities across the country. Other reasons were the growth in population, which had started with the baby boom of the 1950s and the increase in unwed teenage mothers. By the 1980s mounting drug use had added to the problem. By the end of that decade, housing for homeless AIDS victims had become a concern.

By the beginning of the 1990s, all the elements of homelessness that we are faced with today were in place. The debate between helping the victims and coddling the freeloaders became more and more heated. Today, the controversy is intense, and the very identity of the homeless has become a major part of it.

At the core of this controversy are two questions: Who are the homeless? Why are they homeless?

3

TODAY'S HOMELESS: WHO THEY ARE AND WHY

"There's homeless people everywhere. . . . They don't know how many men are living up here by the zoo. Women too. They're chased out of the subway, chased out of Central Park. They make their little huts down by the river and the city burns them down. Some of them spend the whole night on the ferry that goes out to Staten Island. They go back and forth all night because, if they get off, they'll be arrested."

Interview with Mrs. Alice Washington,
a formerly homeless AIDS patient[1]

Alice Washington was a high-school graduate with a job when she contracted AIDS from her husband. A short time later he began to beat her, and she left him, taking her children with her. She then developed cancer. When she was thirty-nine, she and her children were moved by the city of New York into a shelter with no running water. For the next four years she and her children lived in city shelters.

Richard Kreimer of Morristown, New Jersey, was an unemployed man who hung out in the Morristown Public Library. He was aggressive toward other library patrons, and he smelled very bad. When the library tried to bar him from the premises, Richard Kreimer sued. He won his case and the right to spend as much time as he wanted in the library. He was also awarded $150,000 in damages. Logically, Mr. Kreimer now had enough money to rent, or even to buy, an apartment or a house. But he chose not to, insisting that he had a right to live however he wanted—and to continue being homeless if he preferred.[2]

IDENTIFYING THE HOMELESS

Both Alice Washington and Richard Kreimer were homeless. Obviously, their circumstances were very different. "The homeless population is diverse," sociologist Joel Blau reminds us. He adds that it is "mobile" and that, "for understandable reasons, homeless people may not always tell the truth about themselves."[3] Those reasons might include shame or embarrassment. Sometimes there are crimes to conceal, warrants out for nonpayment of alimony, or debt collectors to avoid.

Because the homeless are so varied, move around so much, and sometimes lie, an accurate count of them is hard to come by. Despite this, the various public and private agencies that deal with the problem of homelessness generally agree on the makeup of homeless subgroups and on the percentage of each subgroup among the unsheltered population as a whole. That's what the U. S. Interagency Council on the Homeless—working with the

Department of Housing and Urban Development (HUD) Office of Community Planning and Development—concluded in its 1993–1994 report, a section of which defined the characteristics of the homeless population.

The study looked at recent national surveys as well as local surveys in many different parts of the country. The nationwide effort relied on cooperation from "more than 14,000 representatives of state and local governments, not-for-profit providers of services and housing, advocates for homeless people, economic and community development leaders, educators and social-service professionals, and currently and formerly homeless individuals and families."[4] Seventeen forums were held throughout the country and were attended by some 10,000 individuals concerned with homelessness. HUD Secretary Henry G. Cisneros sent out letters and questionnaires to 12,000 organizations and individuals involved with the problem. Some 400 homeless people in shelters were interviewed and filled out questionnaires. The Department of Veterans Affairs provided data from interviews with thousands of homeless war veterans.

All these data combined indicated that about 75 percent of homeless people are "single, unattached adults, unaccompanied by children."[5] Their average age is about thirty-five. Among the adult homeless there are five times as many men as women.

The evidence is sketchy, but somewhere between 9 and 39 percent of these adults spent some time in foster care as children. Some 30 to 45 percent of homeless men served in the armed forces.

About 10 percent of them were war veterans suffering from post–traumatic stress disorder (PTSD), a recurring condition related to the horror experienced in combat, which causes "nightmares or flashbacks . . . psychic numbness . . . difficulty sleeping and concentrating . . ."[6] and can result in intense anxiety affecting the ability of the sufferer to function.

Families with children make up another 20 percent of the homeless population. Four out of five of these families are headed by a single mother. A U. S. Department of Education study found that "as many as one third of homeless children may not be attending school on a regular basis."[7]

According to the National Coalition for the Homeless, "families with children are among the fastest growing segments of the homeless population."[8] Significantly, many of the single mothers of these children are themselves the children of single mothers. However, these single-parent families are driven to homelessness by a variety of conditions, which include abusive relationships, inability to pay rent, lack of affordable housing, and loss of welfare benefits.

MINORITIES AT RISK

There is some disagreement as to the racial mix of homeless people, but there is no doubt that minorities are overrepresented among them. The 1993–1994 Interagency Council study reported that 40 percent of homeless persons were African American. A 1996 survey of twenty-nine cities by the U. S. Conference of Mayors put the figure at 57 percent. It also said that 10 percent were Hispanic, 2 percent Native American, and 1 percent Asian.

One reason for the high numbers of blacks among the homeless is that roughly one third of all African Americans are poor. Some 2.5 million black families live below the poverty level. They exist, in effect, on the edge of homelessness. They are often forced to live in slums. The jobless rate is high. *The African American Market Report* puts "the national unemployment rate for African Americans at 12.6%, roughly double that for U. S. workers as a whole."[9] Between 1978 and 1995 the percentage of African American families with no earners increased from 10 to 19 percent.

African Americans also have 32 percent more children than white Americans. Some 64 percent of black babies are born out of wedlock, compared with 18 percent of white babies. The time, money, and emotional pressures on unemployed single mothers are a major factor contributing to homelessness.

The shortage of low-cost rental housing in cities like New York and Boston, which have large African American populations, is another race-related factor. In rural areas the homeless are much more likely to be white. However, there are a significant number of Hispanics and Native Americans among the migrant farm laborers who crisscross those rural areas in search of work.

RURAL CASUALTIES

Because the homeless tend to move around so much, it's hard to determine how many of them can be classified as rural as opposed to urban. Many people in rural regions who lose their homes migrate to cities to seek jobs and shelter and to take advantage of the support services offered. Cities with populations over 50,000 have larger tax bases, and

Like some rural homeless, this family (photographed in 1989) moves around from place to place in search of work. Some homeless people go to cities, where there are more services available.

thus can finance support services for the homeless that small farming communities, hard hit by an economic crisis, cannot.

Not all of the homeless have left these rural areas, and many small towns have funded homeless shelters and soup kitchens. They have to struggle, however, to keep up with the increasing demand for such services. Across the country from Maine to California, other rural homeless sleep in their cars or trucks, under railroad bridges, or in caves.

Homeless migrant workers still follow the crops just as they did during the Depression. There are still men riding the boxcars and sleeping under the stars. And among them there are still those whose homelessness problem exists side-by-side with alcoholism, drug addiction, mental illness, or a combination of such conditions.

THE MENTALLY ILL

The 1994 report of the U. S. Interagency Council on the Homeless estimated that "up to one-third of the adult homeless population have severe mental illness."[10] This includes the slightly more than 400,000 patients released from mental institutions between 1960 and 1980. Most were let out because of the Community Mental Health Center Act, resulting in an 80 percent decline in the number of patients in such state facilities.

When the act was passed in 1963, the plan was to set up 2,000 community centers to provide outpatient services and medication to those suffering from nondangerous mental illnesses. The U. S. General Accounting Office reports that fewer than 800 centers were actually opened. With not nearly enough services to help the mentally ill keep their SRO quarters, or to provide group housing, this segment of the homeless population was soon a highly visible presence on the streets. Confused, bumping into people, mumbling to themselves, or shouting, they have become the most noticeable homeless.

Their mental condition combines with their homelessness to interfere with their washing, shaving, and changing clothes. Their confusion increases, and it becomes harder for them to deal with people, even family members or close friends, let alone the general public. They remain homeless over longer periods of time than others do. The National Coalition for the Homeless points out that "they encounter more barriers to employment, tend to be in poorer physical health, and have more contact with the legal system" than do other homeless people.[11]

Mental illness among the homeless is often complicated by alcoholism and drug abuse. However, not all of those without permanent shelter who are addicted to alcohol or drugs are mentally ill. Nor can it be fairly said that such addictions will lead to homelessness. The vast majority of people with alcohol and drug problems do not end up living on the street.

The Interagency Council on the Homeless report cited evidence that "about half of the single homeless adult population suffers from substance abuse problems."[12] The National Coalition for the Homeless believes that the Council's figure is twice as large as it should be because the surveys on which it is based "greatly over-represented long-term shelter users and single men" who were more likely than other homeless people to have such problems.[13] A 1995 report by the U. S. Bureau of Primary Health Care found that only 22 percent of homeless people suffered from addictions to alcohol or drugs. But that figure only includes those who sought health care.

Even the lowest estimates demonstrate that drinking and drug use are serious conditions that add to the problems of homelessness. Simply put, money used to support such addictions can't be used to pay rent. Recent studies show that less than half of homeless alcohol and drug addicts are being treated for their conditions. There are long waiting lists at treatment centers, and many who need help simply give up hope of receiving it.

THE DOOMED RUNAWAYS

The pressures of homelessness strike hardest at children. Those children living in homeless families suffer "serious emotional and developmental problems that can persist long after their families find permanent housing."[14] During their homelessness these children often live in a dangerous world populated by drug pushers and torn by turf wars.

Not all homeless children, however, live in family situations. Many between the ages of twelve and eighteen—and some even younger—are runaways living on their own. Some are fleeing abusive home situations, while others run away from home to avoid traditional parental discipline. Some of these runaway youths, both male and female, end up prostituting themselves. Frequently pimps become substitute parent figures. The pimps often introduce

Runaway teens are one of the most at-risk groups of homeless people. These two streeet kids call the streets of New York City's East Village their home.

them to drugs. Even if the young people manage to break away from prostitution, they are caught up in the drug culture of the homeless population.

LEGAL AND ILLEGAL IMMIGRANTS

Recently the homeless population has included more and more immigrants. Often they have slipped into the country illegally from Mexico or Central America, or have been brought from mainland China to work as farm laborers or in sweatshop clothing factories. But since they must avoid immigration authorities, they can't hold jobs. Without money they join the ranks of the street people.

In addition, as Ruth Sidel, professor of Sociology at Hunter College, points out, "Over the past decade and a half [1981–1996] the United States has experienced a massive surge of immigration."[15] This population is in the country legally and was entitled until recently to the same social services as others. This changed when President Clinton signed into law the Welfare Reform Act of 1996. The act, according to a 1997 report by the Children's Defense Fund, resulted in a "sweeping ban on benefits for legal immigrants, children and adults alike."[16] Whole immigrant households were denied benefits from programs like Temporary Assistance for Needy Families (TANF) and Medicaid. The act has pushed more and more immigrants into homelessness.

NO JOB, NO RENT, NO HOME

Other government programs that some advocates believe have served to increase the ranks of the homeless are trade deals like the North American Fair Trade Agreement (NAFTA). President Clinton claims that thanks to such programs, "Today 12 million American jobs are supported by exports."[17] But critics protest that these policies have also resulted in the loss of many American jobs to cheap labor in other countries. Nobody knows exactly how many people have become homeless because of the export of jobs.

Another practice that may have resulted in job loss and homelessness is downsizing, or the mass firing of workers by factories, banks, corporations, and many branches of government. Throughout the 1990s, large-scale layoffs affected tens of thousands of workers at a time. Automation and efforts to hold down costs by introducing more efficient ways to use smaller work forces have driven many who were let go to take lower-paying jobs in service industries such as fast-food chains. This in turn has deprived people on welfare of the chance to supplement their incomes with part-time jobs in such areas and driven them into homelessness.

CIRCUMSTANCE AND DEATH

Other homeless subgroups include ex-convicts and people with physical illnesses. Their circumstances are often the cause of their homelessness, and may also be why they continue to be homeless.

Ex-convicts find that employers shy away from hiring them. Without a job they can't afford to pay rent. When they do go on job interviews, their homelessness prevents them from leaving an address or phone number where they can be contacted for work. Forced into municipal shelters, they sometimes use prison skills to prey on other homeless people. The cycle they are caught in frequently lands them back in prison, where they at least have a home.

Those who are physically ill face a different set of pressures related to homelessness. They are most often among the 41 million Americans who do not have health insurance. When illness strikes, their savings can be quickly wiped out. Many become homeless as a result.

The most common diseases found among the homeless are tuberculosis, diabetes, AIDS, and hypertension (high blood pressure). These diseases are aggravated by exposure and stress. Sufferers grow weaker and less able to muster the energy to seek permanent shelter. Often they die.

Indeed, the life expectancy of the homeless is twenty years less than that of the population at large. Their death rate is three times as high. They are buried in paupers' graves, homeless still.

THE HOMELESS THEMSELVES ARE RESPONSIBLE

"The homeless . . . are homeless, you might say, by choice."

President Ronald Reagan[1]

President Ronald Reagan was an early voice among those who questioned the claim by champions of the homeless that conditions of poverty are the main cause of the problem. According to these critics, it is the behavior of the homeless themselves that causes and perpetuates their condition. "Many of the homeless have willingly chosen to be homeless and chosen to steal, take drugs, and abandon their families for a life free of ties and responsibilities," is how writer Theodore Pappas summed up this view.[2]

Those who agree point to cases like that of Mrs. Jacqueline Williams of Washington, D.C. Mrs. Williams was a homeless mother of fourteen children whom authorities had placed in a welfare motel. She was selected to appear on *The Phil Donahue Show* along with the mayor of Washington. The embarrassing question facing the mayor was why the city of Washington had not provided adequate housing for Mrs. Williams and her children.

Viewer response to the show demanded a home for the Williams family. City agencies reacted to the pressure, and Mrs. Williams and her children were placed in a house that had been fixed up, painted, and given new bathroom and kitchen fixtures. The city paid the rent each month.

A year went by. City inspectors checked on the house, and they found that it wasn't fit to be lived in. The kitchen and bathroom fixtures and much of the plumbing had been ripped out. Cabinets and furniture were gone. There was trash all over the house. The windows and doors had been vandalized, and there was graffiti on the walls. They found that the children had been continually neglected and abused. Those children under the age of eighteen were taken away from Mrs. Williams and put in foster care.[3]

A LACK OF WILL

The case of Mrs. Williams may be an extreme one, but there is evidence that providing housing does not solve the problems of homeless people who lack the will to help themselves. A study by the New York City Commission on the homeless reported that "fully half of all homeless families placed in permanent housing returned to the shelter system."[4] In Washington, D. C., there were similar return rates.

A California study of 400 homeless families found that they were often not as poor as families with homes and that their not having shelter was a result of such factors as personal problems and family conflicts, not just poverty. A report by the Health Care for the Homeless Project found that "the immense majority of the extremely poor manage to secure housing."[5] Those who object to putting the blame on society for homelessness conclude from this evidence that the problem is less a matter of lack of affordable housing and more often a lack of will on the part of the homeless to improve their condition.

"If poverty is the cause of homelessness," they ask, "why are there so very many poor people in this country who are not homeless?"[6] They add that "it is not true that we are all just a paycheck away from homelessness" because the size of the homeless population doesn't grow or shrink according to whether the economy is doing well or badly.[7] The claim is made that there is "significant evidence that some of the homeless have never worked, that many work only sporadically, and that most have not worked for far longer than they have been homeless."[8]

Perhaps the foremost sponsor of the idea that personal irresponsibility is at the root of all homelessness is the nation's most listened-to radio commentator, Rush Limbaugh. He is a powerful force behind the way that Americans regard homelessness today. He tells his listeners that "most of what you hear about the homeless is fraudulent."[9]

Limbaugh believes that this fraud is deliberate and that the homeless are "being exploited" to further

Radio talk-show host Rush Limbaugh is a strong voice that is often heard in the debate on the homeless. He feels that homelessness is "tied to a lack of personal responsibility and a...decline in respect for the traditional American values of hard work, self-reliance, and respect for the law."

"a liberal agenda."[10] He says homelessness is "tied to a lack of personal responsibility and a generation-long decline in respect for the traditional American values of hard work, self-reliance, and respect for the law."[11] He accuses advocates for the homeless of being power-hungry and of wanting "to build up a giant network of government programs that employ their friends. . . ." He sneers at them as "the leaders of the alms race" and calls them "Poverty Pimps."[12]

Limbaugh challenges the statistics used by advocates for the homeless. As an example, he cites a speech by Mitch Snyder, a formerly homeless man who became a spokesperson for the movement to obtain federal government help for the homeless. Snyder, who has since died, claimed that forty-five homeless people die every second. Limbaugh "ran the numbers and found that for that to be true, some 23 million homeless people would die in America every year."[13] This would, of course, be many times the number of homeless people living in America over a twelve-month period.

QUALITY OF LIFE ISSUES

One of Limbaugh's concerns, shared by others who believe that the homeless must take responsibility for their plight, is the effect of homelessness on the quality of life for the community at large. When ordinary people have to step over alcoholics and drug addicts to get up the subway steps or into the entrances of their workplaces every day, their compassion is soon worn away. Mental-health experts fear that the hard shell most people would develop may carry over to the other relationships in their lives.

In warmer weather, observed John Leo in *U. S. News & World Report,* the homeless hang out in the parks. As a result, "Sandboxes become urinals. Swings are broken. Every park bench seems to be owned by a permanently curled-up dozing alcoholic or perhaps a street schizophrenic." Soon there are what Los Angeles and Washington, D.C., have called "dead parks."[14] These are parks that are shared by the homeless and drug pushers. Ordinary people no longer go to them, let alone bring their children.

Stuart D. Bykofsky, writing in *Newsweek,* had run out of sympathy for the homeless. "I don't know, exactly, when they got the *right* to live on the street," he protested. "I don't know, exactly, when I *lost* the right to walk through town without being pestered by panhandlers. . . . I am fed up with the trash they bring into my neighborhood. The pools of urine in apartment-house lobbies disgust me. I am fed up with picking my way down sidewalks blocked by plastic milk crates, stepping over human forms sprawled on steam gratings. . . ."[15]

Justifiably or not, many people are afraid of the homeless. The most visible homeless are the street people. They tend to be unkempt, are sometimes unwashed, and sometimes smell bad. Too often they are drunk or high on drugs, or they are mentally ill and behave in irrational ways.

People fear for themselves in the streets, on subways, and in public libraries and other enclosed places. They are afraid they will be mugged, held up, or molested. They fear even more for their children when a homeless person behaves irrationally only a few feet from a playground. This fear is a major

At one time Tompkins Square Park in New York City fit the description of a dead park, a place that seemed to have been taken over by homeless people and drug addicts. The park was considered unusable by the general public and their children.

assault on the quality of life. It can interfere with people's ability to function. Some believe that such fear eats away at the very soul of a community.

OTHER ISSUES

Negative attitudes toward the homeless often stem from the way in which other problems afflicting society are viewed. For instance, not everybody sees alcoholism as a disease. To some it is simply drunkenness, a deliberate unwillingness to be a responsible and functioning person. Drug addicts are regarded not as sick people, but as objects of scorn. "Why don't they 'Just Say No'?" is the question asked by disgusted citizens. There is resentment over a war on drugs that cost the American people $120 billion over a four-year period, with the costs still mounting. Why should the average citizen taxpayer have to pay for sheltering self-indulgent addicts in addition to the burden of fighting the drug plague?

Many people believe that the mentally ill should not have been released from institutions. The homeless among them in particular, they say, cannot function on their own. Even if they are not really dangerous to a neighborhood, their bizarre behavior makes people ill at ease.

A breakdown in family values is seen as one of the key links in the chain of behavior leading to homelessness. The homeless are identified with the loosening of moral standards that has led to an increasing number of teenage pregnancies, a mounting divorce rate, a widespread decrease in parental authority, adolescent drug and alcohol abuse, and a lowering of educational standards and performance by students. Lax discipline, reduced respect for authority, and a permissive atmosphere that encourages dependency are all viewed as responsible for many of the ills of society. These factors provide the push that begins the slide into homelessness.

"TOUGH LOVE"

Rush Limbaugh, believing that the homeless have been coddled, thinks that the best way to deal with homelessness is through "tough love."[16] This means that there should be no benefits for addicts or alcoholics who don't seek treatment and attend treatment programs regularly. There should be no welfare for unmarried teenage mothers unless they go to school. There should be no welfare for other single parents unless they find jobs or enroll in job training programs.

It may also mean a "boot camp" approach, in which the self-defeating attitudes of the homeless person come under constant attack. The idea is that people can only help themselves by giving up the defenses meant to support—but really used to hide— their low self-image. Group pressure is brought to bear on individuals to shape up, learn to walk tall, and build up the toughness necessary to cope with a world that nobody said was going to be easy.

A spokesperson for a shelter program for homeless men that takes a tough-love approach puts it this way: "If a guy gets a job, the housing pretty much can take care of itself. . . . Going to work, even picking up leaves or sweeping the streets— anybody who says that's a dead end doesn't have any understanding of the difference between the work culture—the free-enterprise culture—and the welfare culture."[17] This is also the view of those who think the best chance of ending homelessness is to substitute workfare programs (in which the homeless do community service in exchange for benefits) for public assistance.

WELFARE CHEATS AND HUSTLERS

Tough-love advocates view the homeless as divided between the shiftless, lazy, and self-defeated on the one hand, and those who have learned to manipulate the system on the other. They point to well-documented cases of welfare fraud to support their view. Among such cases are homeless individuals who collected three or four public-assistance checks a month for years under different names, or in neighboring states. Such fraud has been so common that Ronald Reagan, when he was president, expressed outrage at "welfare queens" living the high life by feasting at the trough of government aid programs.

Some of the homeless have learned how to manipulate the system in a variety of other ways. They will get free clothing from various charities and then sell the clothes at thrift shops. They will make a daily circuit of government agencies for handouts, sometimes receiving vouchers that they can swap with other homeless people for cash for liquor or drugs. Some engage in petty theft—an apple from an outdoor fruit stand, or items from a drugstore or supermarket.

A volunteer at a Coalition for the Homeless feeding program up the block from Grand Central Terminal in New York City recalls just how clever some of the homeless men who lined up there could be. The street was dark and lined with doorways. The men would queue up for a sandwich, a container of milk, and an apple at ten o'clock at night. After awhile the volunteer became aware that he was handing out food to the same men over and over again. After they got their food, the men would slide into a darkened doorway and merge with the line near the front. They would find a spaced-out addict or alcoholic to walk in front of. If the volunteer insisted that they already had their ration, they would cajole, plead, and talk about bringing food to their kids, all the while not moving so that the line was being held up and the waiting men would start to grumble. Usually it was easier to hand out another sandwich than argue. Later, after the night's food had run out, the volunteer might see the extra sandwich being sold to someone at the end of the line who hadn't received one.

That is only one of many scams the homeless employ. They are clever, which always raises the question of why, if they are so clever, can they not find and hold a job? The answer, say their critics, is that they simply do not want to work.

SOCIETY IS
RESPONSIBLE

". . . I think it grieves the heart of God when human beings created in his image treat other human beings like filthy rags."
Father Glenworth Miles, pastor to the homeless[1]

There are many causes of homelessness. Heading the list, according to advocates for those without permanent shelter, is the lack of affordable housing. It's a matter of arithmetic, they say: too many low-income people and not enough available low-rental apartments and low-cost houses.

The National Coalition for the Homeless offers these figures from a 1995 study by the Center on Budget and Policy Priorities: "Between 1973 and 1993, 2.2 million low-rent units disappeared from the market," while "the number of low-income renters increased by 4.7 million." Today, according to the Coalition, "the gap between the number of affordable housing units and the number of people needing them has created a housing crisis for poor people."[2]

A recent U. S. Department of Housing and Urban Development study confirms this. It found that "almost 95% of those with worst case housing needs paid over half of their income for housing."[3] According to the U. S. Conference of Mayors, waiting periods for housing in 1996 averaged nineteen months for those in need of assistance. In September 1997, *The New York Times* reported that "48 percent of renters in New York State were unable to afford the estimated fair market rent for a one-bedroom apartment, $687, and 54 percent were unable to afford a two-bedroom rent, $796."[4] Helen Dunlap, president of the National Low Income Housing Coalition, sees this as evidence that "you can be working a great number of hours in a steady job and still not be able to afford a place to live."[5]

Those concerned with homelessness blame the shortage of low-cost housing on local, state, and federal policies that cater to the middle class and the wealthy at the expense of the poor. The federal government has cut back on its public housing programs by 25 percent over the past several years. During the 1980s some 40,000 vouchers were provided to those in need of assistance to help them pay rent. In 1996 not one such voucher was issued. "The federal government has essentially conceded defeat in its decades-long drive to make housing affordable to low-income Americans," concluded Jason DeParle in *The New York Times*.[6]

At the same time, middle-class and upper-income homeowners are receiving more housing help from the government than in past years. They get this help in the form of mortgage interest deductions and property tax deductions. More than two thirds of this money is saved by families who earn above $75,000 a year. The landlords of poor people may profit from these tax breaks, but the savings are rarely passed along to the renters.

On the local level, in cities like New York and Boston, real estate developers have been receiving tax abatements and other help to build middle-income and luxury apartment houses. This follows the tearing down of single-room-occupancy hotels (SROs), which resulted in homelessness for many mentally ill people. Other landlords have walked away from decaying buildings rather than spend the money to make the repairs necessary to keep them livable. City governments seize such buildings as payment for the taxes owed on them, but do not restore them.

Catch 22: Food or Shelter?

Poverty—joblessness and all the ills that go along with being out of work—combines with the lack of affordable housing stock to push people into homelessness and keep them there. Consider the case of Martha and Charles and their three children. When Charles lost his job, the family was left with enough money for food or shelter, but not both. They were forced to move into a homeless shelter.

The five-member family was assigned a 13- by 16-foot (4- by 5-meter) cubicle. They shared the bathroom with other shelter residents. The two older children, both girls, complained that there was no curtain on the shower. It was "like living in a shoe box," they said.[7]

The family's situation was not uncommon, say advocates for the homeless. Indeed, it was not as bad as some. Many shelters are unsafe places where

Government-run shelters for the homeless are often dangerous as well as poorly equipped, due to a lack of funds for proper policing and supplies. This women's shelter in Washington, D.C., seems to at least be clean, even if some women have to sleep on the floor in a hallway.

theft and crimes of violence, including rape, are nightly occurrences. Many homeless people refuse to go to the shelters. They feel safer on the streets. Why, they ask, do authorities turn a deaf ear to pleas for effective policing of the shelters?

NO WORK FOR THE HOMELESS

Lack of safety is only one of the harsh effects of homelessness. Billy Easton, executive director of the New York State Tenants and Neighbors Coalition, points out that "if someone doesn't have a stable home, it has a terrible impact on every other area of their lives—their ability to work, the ability of their children to stay in school."[8] In a very real sense, being homeless can be an alternative school teaching all the wrong lessons to children, as well as a full-time career with little or no pay for adults.

Advocates view single adults without children, roughly three quarters of the homeless, as trapped by the lack of job opportunities. Often they either don't have the necessary education and job skills, or their abilities have become useless because of the advances in modern technology. There is a shortage of both training and retraining for them.

If they are lucky, they can land minimum-wage jobs. But such jobs are seen as dead ends, offering little chance for homeless people to better themselves. Others become vagrants who travel from place to place picking crops for low wages, or they join the ranks of urban street people who survive on public assistance and panhandling. Our society, say advocates, offers few other opportunities for the homeless.

They add that it's not that the homeless don't want to work, it's that not having a home makes it incredibly hard to look for a job. Grooming oneself, shaving, and washing are problems. So is keeping clothes cleaned and pressed.

Lack of transportation can make it hard to get to a job interview. Employment applications, which require a permanent address and phone number, can't be filled out properly. Even if a shelter phone number is listed, chances are that messages will not be passed on to the applicant. The homeless are often shifted around from shelter to shelter. Job offers do not follow them.

After a while they sink into depression. They stop hoping. Perhaps they start drinking to blot out their misery. Perhaps they take to drugs. Feeling hopeless and not even worthy of having a home, they use addictive substances more and more. The 1993–1994 Interagency Council study concluded that "the experience of homelessness itself may trigger heavy drinking and drug use by people who have not had such problems in the past and may prompt renewed substance abuse by people whose earlier problems had been under control."[9]

THE PLIGHT OF SINGLE MOTHERS

By not providing training, treatment, and adequate health care, say advocates, society dooms the homeless to remain homeless. Without help they can't even get a foot on the first rung of the ladder to a job, a home, and a good life. This is particularly true for heads of single-parent households—usually young women, too often teenagers.

These young women may also fall into the trap of substance abuse. Motherhood places many additional pressures on them. Child care itself can be a full-time job in the environment of welfare hotels and homeless shelters. It is necessary to constantly be on guard against petty thievery, sex molesters, batterers, drugs, and the violence connected with drugs. In this environment, health is a constant concern. Children become ill from lead paint or asbestos in the decaying old hotels or shelters where they are housed. Sometimes they must sleep on the floors or desks of government offices when shelter can't be found for them for the night.

How does a person feed his or her children properly on a limited budget? ask those who work with the homeless. Living in a place without cooking facilities, a young mother may watch helplessly as her children gobble down fast foods with little nutritional value. Later, she may sit in a free clinic for hours waiting for a prescription for a child's stomachache.

Her ability to look for a job is also hampered by time-consuming dealings with the welfare bureaucracy she must depend on for even minimal needs. She must go from federal to state to city agencies to collect food stamps, health-care vouchers, welfare checks, aid for her children, or social security if she or her child has a disability. She must register her children in school, then re-register them when the city moves her from one homeless facility to another, and then shuttle between schools to achieve the transfers. The process is physically wearing and emotionally exhausting.

IMMIGRANTS, MIGRANTS, AND MINORITIES

These problems are even worse for certain subgroups of the homeless. In addition to lack of shelter, both legal and illegal immigrants often must deal with problems of communicating in English. This is particularly hard on immigrant children, who may be moved from school to school, never receiving ongoing English language training.

Migrants looking for farmwork often meet hostility in small towns that view them as possible welfare burdens at best and dangerous drifters at worst. The mentally ill homeless must function in a cloud of confusion. Those with physical illnesses are dependent on overcrowded medical facilities and often receive inadequate treatment.

The minority homeless—African Americans, Native Americans, Latinos, Asians, and others—must deal with bigotry in addition to all the other problems of being homeless. Black men are more often hassled by police than other homeless people. They may feel that they are more often shunned and ignored. They know that race has played its part in causing their problems.

Study after study since the 1950s has confirmed the relationship between poverty and race. Back then segregation was a fact of life for African Americans. It was legal and enforced in the South. While not an official policy in the rest of the country, it was *de facto*—a matter of blacks being kept out of certain neighborhoods both by their lack of earning power and by agreement among homeowners, real estate agents, and banks.

De facto segregation is illegal today, but it still exists in many parts of our nation. What this has meant is that many middle-income as well as low-income black families have been kept separated from the white population. According to the October 1995 *African American Market Report*, "a survey of 85,652 applications made to banks and other lending institutions in 1992 revealed that African Americans were 2.86 times more likely to be turned down for a home mortgage than whites."

There was—and still is—racial discrimination in jobs. One result is that in those communities where blacks live the earnings are lower than in comparable white communities. This means that the tax base that supports the local school system is lower. Inevitably, say African American leaders, this has led to inferior education for minority children.

The "black poverty cycle," first spelled out more than forty years ago, works like this: Poor black families dependent on low-paying jobs cluster in low-rent or low-cost housing areas. These areas are traditionally shortchanged by local governments when it comes to crime prevention, sanitation, and schools.

College is usually not an option for African American children who live in these areas because most families can't afford it. The children grow up and take low-paying jobs which force them to live in substandard housing areas, where their children in turn will receive inferior educations. Many black families have broken out of this cycle, but for those that have not, drugs, crime, and downsizing have made their situation even harder to overcome.

An accident, emergency, lingering illness, the loss of a job, or domestic problems may push such an African American family over the edge into homelessness. The family may end up in a shelter or a welfare hotel. If they are lucky, after a year or two, the authorities may help them find permanent housing again.

But they are not always so lucky. Mrs. Alice Washington thought that maybe her luck had changed when she and her children were moved out of the Martinique, a New York welfare hotel notorious for drugs and violence, and into an apartment in the Bronx. "I was wrong," she soon realized. "Instead of putting two of us [from the Martinique] here, two of us there, two others over there, they kept us all together and they put us all in places where the drugs were bad already. So you took a place of death and added more death, and more danger, and this was intentional and it was spiteful and it was a conscious plan."[10]

Many homeless African Americans share Mrs. Washington's bitterness and her conviction that they are victims of a society that is deliberately harsh in its treatment of them. Some of their advocates agree that society has much to answer for. Robert Hayes, a former executive director of the National Coalition for the Homeless, sums up homelessness as the result of "a cruel economy, an unresponsive government, [and] a festering value system"[11]—all areas in which the more fortunate must share responsibility.

THE DUTY OF GOVERNMENT

"Even though I quit school at sixteen, I didn't want to stay a drop-out. I wanted to pay my own way and not depend on any money from the government. But when I had Jemma, I had to quit my job . . . and I had to go on welfare. . . . I couldn't afford any baby-sitters and Jemma never got off the wait-list for day care. . . . I couldn't find a decent apartment that I could even hope to pay for with my check. . . . Jemma and me ended up at a shelter.

"I just want to take care of my baby, but we always get some sort of bad luck. I know there is supposed to be help out there, but I can't seem to get it. Why can't the government help me?"

Lisa, a homeless single mother[1]

Champions of the homeless believe that government—federal, state, and local—has a responsibility to help people who, like Lisa and her daughter Jemma, lack shelter. They agree with President Franklin D. Roosevelt's Second Bill of Rights speech in 1944, which proclaimed "the right of every family to a decent home."[2] Reaffirming that right, the National Coalition for the Homeless—the largest and oldest national organization dealing with the problem—proclaims that its purpose "is to *end* homelessness."[3]

It is not just a problem for those without housing, advocates point out. Rather, homelessness is a growing condition that lowers the quality of life for the nation as a whole. Well-funded government programs, they believe, are the only effective way to wipe it out. Toward this end, these advocates want the government to address the problems of homelessness at their roots.

In Lisa's case this might have meant more effective counseling for her when she decided to quit school at age sixteen. Birth control and birth control information would have been provided to her when it was determined that she was sexually active. After Jemma was born, child care would have been made available so that Lisa would not have had to quit her job and go on welfare.

Government aid could have paid part of the rent for a decent apartment. Follow-up assistance might have gotten her and her baby out of the shelter system, into temporary housing, and then into permanent housing. Providing necessary services could have kept Lisa there until she was able to get her life together, and to hold down the decent-paying job needed to meet her rent.

This is not a fuzzy-headed do-gooder pipe dream. It is what was recommended by the Clinton Administration's 1993–1994 Interagency Council study. The study concluded that "the number of homeless persons on the street and in the shelters is constantly being fed by a stream of poor persons who are precariously housed."[4]

EARLY INTERVENTION PROGRAMS

Specifically, the study recommends what poverty experts call early intervention programs. It is widely agreed these are the keys to preventing home lessness. The programs try to help poor people who are on the brink of losing their housing before it is too late.

Some early intervention governmental programs do exist, but supporters complain that they are underfunded and that many more are needed. This is borne out by a report in *The New York Times* that "renters on welfare continue to be in the most precarious position."[5] They live with the threat of not being able to go on affording a place to live.

A typical case is that of Leslie Crockett, who lost her job in January 1997. She had to go on welfare, but the program paid only part of her rent. When her landlord took her to court, she and her three children faced being thrown out of their apartment.

"I understand that man needs his money," Leslie Crockett said. "He's got a business to run as well. But this is the situation that I'm in. I don't have anyone to take up the slack for me."[6]

FEDERAL AID FOR POOR TENANTS

It is the duty of government, say advocates for the homeless, to take up the slack. Not only that, it is sensible public policy. It is cheaper by far to supplement Leslie Crockett's rent and keep her and her children in their apartment than it is to house them and provide all the services necessary to support them once they are homeless. New York and other major cities have paid $1,000 a week and more to house a four-person family in a welfare hotel. A few hundred dollars a month is all Leslie Crockett needed to pay her rent.

The recommended basis for such payment is that tenants like Leslie Crockett, whether on welfare or working, use 30 percent of their income for rent and the government makes up the difference between that amount and the rent charged by the landlord. The government would ensure that this was a fair market rent. The payment could be in the form of cash or vouchers to the tenant or the landlord.

Government money to provide affordable housing remains the lead item on the advocates' wish list. Although such funding is already available in a variety of forms, advocates insist that it falls far short of what is needed. They would like more federal subsidies (such as grants, loans, and tax relief) for developers who build low-cost housing for low-income earners. They want the federal government to put into action the Interagency Council's suggestion that the Federal National Mortgage Association purchase mortgages or bonds as a means of funding low-rent housing projects.

SQUATTERS AND TAX ABATEMENTS

Presently many cities and states give tax abatements (freedom from paying taxes on the rents they collect for a specified period of time) to developers who create housing that poor people *cannot* afford. Housing advocates want to correct that. They believe that tax abatements should go only to those developments that include 30 to 50 percent low-cost or low-rent housing, or to those builders who will reserve 20 percent of the new housing they build for the homeless. As a condition of tax abatements and other subsidies, they want a proportion of the units built to be SRO units for single homeless men and women, including those with addiction problems and the mentally ill.

They want local governments, such as New York City, to restore the housing stock they own. At present the city government is the largest slum landlord in New York. This is the result of landlords deserting buildings because it doesn't pay to repair them and pay taxes on them. When the city can't—or won't—restore the run-down apartment buildings it has taken over, homeless people often move into them and fix them up themselves. In 1995 and 1996, these people, called squatters, took over several buildings in New York's East Village and did extensive repair work on them. The once-homeless squatters thought they had created homes for themselves, but the city, claiming that the buildings were unsafe, said they must leave.

When the squatters refused to go, the police staged a midnight raid to drive them out. They cordoned off the block and went through the buildings one by one. A squad of helicopters circled overhead, searchlights blazing to light up the rooftops where the squatters were trying to elude the police. The first raid was followed by a second and a third. The police then remained on the blocks they had targeted to make sure the homeless did not return.

Housing advocates question the city's claim that the buildings were unsafe. To the homeless, they point

Trying to protect the interests of the city, its residents, and the homeless themselves, the police drove squatters out of abandoned buildings in New York's East Village in 1996. In 1989, as this picture shows, the homeless had been evicted from nearby Tompkins Square Park. For many people, these actions underscored the need for more services for the homeless.

out, they were safer than the city's shelter system, the welfare hotels, or even some of the apartments the city had provided for the homeless in high-crime areas of the city. The squatters had done considerable work to make the apartments safer than they had been during the period of neglect since the city had taken them over.

If the apartments were unsafe, the advocates say, then the city should have taken steps to fix them rather than evict the squatters. They accuse the city of acting for real estate developers who wanted the property condemned so that the buildings would be torn down by the city. The land could then be sold to the developers and apartment buildings put up with rents far beyond the reach of the homeless and other poor people.

Government should encourage the squatters to restore abandoned buildings, say their spokespersons. If cities will not fix up these buildings themselves, then at the least they should provide tools, materials, and technical assistance to those who are willing to do the work. In a huge city like New York there are tens of thousands of such apartments—enough to house many of the homeless.

SCATTERED SITE HOUSING

Squatters' rights are only one of the issues requiring attention from government agencies. The homeless include a variety of subgroups, each with its own special set of problems. Well-funded programs must be designed for these subgroups, say advocates, and they must be flexible enough to deal with a variety of circumstances.

For example, Lee Kreiling, former director of scattered site housing for the New York Coalition for the Homeless, points out the difficulty of securing housing on the open market for HIV-infected clients. Living in shelters or on the street can be life-threatening for AIDS patients. Because of the damage to their immune systems, they are extremely susceptible to all sorts of diseases.

Scattered site housing was designed to avoid grouping people such as these in the same neighborhood. There are two reasons for this. First, it is important that no single neighborhood feels that it is being singled out as a dumping ground for homeless people with AIDS. Second, the clients do not want to be segregated in that way.

"In general," says Lee Kreiling, "finding housing for the homeless means locating available low-cost units, and that usually means securing apartments in the poorer areas. The people in those neighborhoods say 'look, we've already got our share of poverty problems—crime, drugs, lack of adequate health care, prejudice—so why don't you spread the burden and put these people where the well-off folks live?' The point is valid, but the rents are too high in such places. Scattered site housing isn't a total solution, but it is a step in the right direction. If the government is going to be involved in housing the homeless, it must address such issues. It must provide both monitoring and support for those it helps to house, and it must be prepared to deal with the range of problems which they may have."[7]

FOLLOW-UP PROGRAMS

Follow-up programs to deal with relocated homeless persons are still badly needed. "The failure to recog-

Providing government-subsidized, low-income housing is one way to help ensure that poor people do not become homeless due to rising housing costs. This typical low-income housing development is located in St. Paul, Minnesota.

nize and address the continuing needs of formerly homeless families is a fundamental flaw in existing policy," insisted Ralph da Costa Nunez, president of Homes for the Homeless.[8] Other advocates agree that if government does not fund and activate such programs, many of the persons it has helped will slip back into homelessness.

Government-sponsored programs for job training and retraining, as well as education programs, are needed to make clients self-supporting. Where needed, child care must be supplied to make regular attendance possible for parents. Counseling must be provided to break the cycle in which patterns of homelessness are passed on from one generation to the next.

Housing is only a first step for those with drug and alcohol problems, as well as for the mentally ill, the physically disabled, the sick, and the aged. Each of these groups requires support services, which may include treatment programs, therapy, home-care services, visiting nurse services, transportation to and from medical facilities—a variety of specialized assistance that advocates want the government to provide.

Some of the homeless have earned the right to government services. According to the 1993–1994 Interagency Council study, "approximately 30 to 45 percent of the entire adult male homeless population have served their country in the armed services. In addition," says the study, "approximately 40 percent of all homeless veterans are African American or Hispanic."[9]

The majority are Vietnam War veterans and Gulf War veterans. Some are women. In many cases the war experiences of men and women alike are directly related to their homelessness. Bitterness is widespread among them. They accuse society of neglect and bigotry. Advocates insist that programs that target these groups must not just provide them with housing, but must also deal with correcting the injustices from which they may still be suffering.

WOMEN AND CHILDREN: A GOVERNMENT RESPONSIBILITY

Single-mother households are perhaps most greatly in need of government monitoring and support services. These include counseling and protection for battered women. Local police may have to be alerted. Involvement by a number of different government agencies may be needed to protect them.

Advocates believe that government should set up more effective monitoring and protection of homeless children. Investigations should also ensure that runaways not be returned to homes where they have been abused. When homeless children are taken away from addicted or abusive parents and put in foster homes, there must be oversight to make sure that they are receiving the affection and care they need. Every effort must be made by government agencies to investigate foster parents beforehand so that homeless children are not shunted from one foster home to another.

The health, nutrition, and education of homeless children must be supervised. Government child-welfare agencies should work with teachers and school officials to ensure that present and former homeless children receive the extra help they need because of missing school or being transferred from one school to another. There should be programs to make other students understand their situation so that homeless children don't feel ostracized.

Homeless children often don't have access to washrooms or bathtubs. Sometimes they smell bad. Sometimes they have head lice. Government must wipe out the root causes of such conditions as well as dealing with them where they exist. Advocates say that government programs must be advanced to make others—children, teachers, and adults—understand that the child victims are not to blame for their circumstances.

Fighting NIMBY

Government, say advocates, must deal with the NIMBY (Not In My Back Yard) attitude that so often hinders the rehousing of the homeless. Often necessary services—mental-health treatment centers, drug and alcohol rehabilitation programs, needle exchanges, even feeding programs and deposit-bottle redemption centers frequented by the homeless—are viewed as threatening to a community. The government must demonstrate that such programs are not a danger, and then they must ensure that they are not.

Neighborhoods and communities should be consulted before programs are put in place. Public-relations campaigns should enlist the agreement and active participation of citizens. Ongoing monitoring should deal with any problems that arise. This requires a full-scale commitment by all levels of government and all of the government agencies involved, say supporters of government programs for the homeless.

Finally, they recommend that government be sensitive to the need of the homeless themselves to be actively involved in solving their problems. Experience has taught that the homeless resent being treated as problems to be solved without having any say in the solution. They want to be involved in the decision-making process.

For one thing, these are *their* problems, and they have insights into them that the most well-intentioned service provider cannot have. For another, being involved is an important part of reclaiming lives. More than anyone, the homeless know that there is more to helping them than just putting a roof over their heads. They believe that only the government has the resources to provide the aid needed to end all of the many problems of homelessness.

7
GOVERNMENT PROGRAMS DON'T WORK

". . . Marriage and family prevent poverty. Schooling prevents poverty. Working at almost any job prevents poverty. Individual actions—rather than more generous government expenditures—are required to escape the poverty trap."

Murray Weidenbaum, director
of the Washington University Center
for the Study of American Business[1]

Poverty and homelessness go hand-in-hand. Those who oppose government efforts to deal with homelessness—particularly large federal government spending programs—understand this. Their arguments against government helping the homeless begin with the basic idea that poor people must handle their own problems and not rely on government to solve them.

In this view, homelessness is a result of poverty, and poverty is a consequence of *individual* failure.

Neither poverty nor homelessness is society's fault, but rather the product of an unwillingness to accept personal responsibility. Neither poverty nor homelessness will be cured by government handouts, but only by the individual taking steps to improve his or her own life.

This is the point of view of Mike Elias, who was once homeless himself. Today Mr. Elias runs a shelter for the homeless in Los Angeles. He doesn't believe in coddling those who come to his shelter. Instead, he tries to get them to view themselves as responsible individuals, rather than as victims or dependents of the government.

"I'm saying 'Homeless people, you've got the power within yourselves to get on your feet and get going,'" Elias explains. "And my colleagues in the business are saying, 'No, it's because—' and they list them. They attack the states, the counties, the cities, the federal government, whatever."[2]

The "colleagues" he speaks of are the majority of those who work with the homeless in different ways at different levels of government and in the private sector. Critics view many of their efforts as self-serving, or as part of an attempt to enlarge liberal social programs. Expanding federal aid to the homeless "will only help current and would-be members of the welfare bureaucracy," writes prominent conservative C. Brandon Crocker in the *California Review*.[3]

Two Opposing Views

Critics of the government's role in dealing with homelessness fall more or less into two categories. Some argue that government at all levels—federal, state, and municipal—should not be directly involved. They believe that private charities and already existing services that deal with specific problems such as mental illness and substance abuse are able to handle the problems. Direct government intervention, these critics say, creates dependency, which in turn causes poverty and homelessness to persist.

Others agree with Heritage Foundation scholar Kenneth J. Bierne that "homelessness is a problem whose best solution draws on the strength of decentralized federalism."[4] What this means is that the federal government should discontinue all programs dealing with homelessness and stop oversight of the federal and state programs that it funds. Instead, it should provide block grants to cities and states to administer according to local conditions and needs.

By closing down various agencies and reducing oversight functions, the federal government would save a lot of money. At the same time, local governments would be able to exercise tighter control over their budgets, and this would also save money. "Studies indicate that the characteristics of the homeless population differ significantly from city to city," Bierne points out. He adds: "What is required is not more top-down money, but clear local resolve and the energetic use of existing resources in the affected areas."[5] Much of this thinking is reflected in the federal Welfare Reform Act passed in 1996.

MISSISSIPPI'S WORK FIRST PROGRAM
Federal policies toward homelessness and other social problems, says Jack Kemp, former secretary of

the U. S. Department of Housing and Urban Development, "reward welfare and unemployment at a higher level than working and productivity." They "reward people who stay in public housing more than those who want to move up and out into private housing and homeownership."[6] Myron Magnet of *Fortune* magazine adds that "like gas pumped into a flooded engine, the more help they [government] bestow, the less able do the poor become to help themselves."[7]

In 1993, Mississippi state officials came to the same conclusion. They blamed government handouts for encouraging teenage pregnancy, joblessness, and the other ills associated with homelessness. Donald R. Taylor, executive director of the state's Department of Human Services, concluded that "the problems we have stem more from behavioral poverty than material poverty."[8]

Mississippi launched a trial program called Work First in six counties of the state. It placed 7,000 people who were on welfare in job-search classes. They had to spend at least thirty-five hours a week in these classes, or in a job-training program, or lose their welfare benefits.

Employers were offered incentives to hire welfare clients, including those who were homeless. They paid salaries of only $1.00 an hour for the first six months of employment. The state of Mississippi provided $4.15 an hour to bring these new workers up to the minimum wage.

Larry Temple, the Mississippi state official in charge of the Work First program, pronounced it "wildly successful."[9] The number of welfare cases in the six counties where Work First had been introduced fell by 19 percent in the first year. In the rest of the state the decrease in welfare cases was less than a third as much. More remarkable was the fact that new applications for welfare fell by 65 percent in the Work First counties.

The rules are tough, grants Temple, "but they are for people who are absolutely refusing to go to work to feed their children."[10] When the government cuts off help, the result is to push the homeless and others on welfare into finding jobs. They realize that they aren't useless, that they can hold a job, be productive, and earn a salary. "I thought it was going to be hard, but it wasn't," says Felicia Fields, who was hired by an insurance company after having gone through a Work First job-search class. "And I can say I earned this money," she adds with pride.[11]

INFERIOR HOUSING, OR NONE AT ALL?

Pride is hard to hold onto when a person has no home. Critics of government programs understand this as well as advocates for the homeless do. However, they claim that it is often these very programs that are responsible for a lack of housing for the homeless.

They point out that once there were skid rows with flophouses in every major American city. They are gone now, writes Fordham University Professor Ernest van den Haag, because "politicians, bureaucrats and bleeding hearts" said they weren't clean enough, sanitary enough, didn't offer enough privacy, or didn't provide enough comforts or conveniences for their homeless tenants. "The former customers," he points out, "now have to sleep on the street. In effect the government has decided that it is better for people to have no roof over their head than to live in places that do not have hot water."[12]

Government regulations, say the critics, make it impossible to build affordable housing for the homeless. Space, windows, heating, electrical, plumbing, and other requirements make it nearly impossible for a builder to put up units that can be rented cheaply enough for the homeless to afford them. Nor can old buildings be repaired to measure up to government standards cheaply enough to hold the rents down. Professor van den Haag claims that "the government . . . refuses to recognize that the street is the actual alternative. So do the many advocates for the homeless."[13]

GOVERNMENT DISCOURAGES BUILDERS

A landlord who tries to rent an apartment not up to government standards can be fined, and may face rent strikes, civil suits, and prosecutions by the city, state, or federal government. On the other hand, a landlord who conforms to the rules is prevented from charging what it costs to comply with the many building codes, laws, and ordinances that regulate housing.

Developers and builders are driven up the wall by the mixed messages they receive from the government. First they are encouraged to create low-rent housing with offers of low-interest loans and tax abatements. But then they are met with licensing and permit requirements and costs, inspections, reinspections, hearings for waivers, and a host of other conditions that add up to lengthy delays. Sacramento developer Angelo Tsakopoulos estimates that these delays "add at least 15 percent to the cost of housing."[14]

Another California developer, Bob Reeder, blames government zoning requirements that limit construction for the shortage of housing. He blames "constraints on density"—how many houses can be built on a particular parcel of land—for "driving up home costs."[15] The result is that only high-rises can be built to house the homeless, and they can be built only with cheap materials and cost-cutting methods, which ensure that they will be the slums of tomorrow.

RENT CONTROL HURTS THE HOMELESS

Another government program that adversely affects the homeless, say critics, is rent control. It was begun during World War II with the Emergency Wartime Residential Rent Control Act. The purpose of the act was to prevent landlords from forcing out longtime tenants in order to let apartments to high-paid war-plant workers at excessive rents.

After the war just about every city except New York did away with rent control. In the 1970s, however, when inflation began driving rents up, it was restored in Boston and other Massachusetts cities, Newark and other New Jersey cities, on Long Island, in Washington, D.C., and in many areas of California. By 1993, more than 200 cities in the United States had rent control. It applied to roughly 20 percent of the nation's rental units.

"Rent control has visibly aggravated homelessness and can only be expected to do worse in the future," declares William Tucker, author of *The Excluded Americans: Homelessness and Housing Policies*. He says that rent control at the local level has made housing "one of the most highly regulated industries in the country." According to Tucker, "an analysis of the rates of homelessness in 50 major cities across the country shows that rent control is the only factor that is associated with high rates of homelessness."[16]

A boon to those who already have apartments and a bane to landlords, rent control harms the homeless because it discourages developers from building low-income housing. Builders don't want to put up housing that rent control will prevent them from renting at what the builders consider a reasonable profit. Also, builders look to the future and foresee a time when rent hikes granted under rent control will not keep pace with maintenance expenses.

At the same time, tenants who benefit from rent control are reluctant to give up their apartments. The result is that by not allowing the rental market to adjust itself according to the law of supply and demand, rent control ensures that the need for low-rent housing far exceeds the units available.

As for the homeless, by discouraging the construction of low-rent housing, rent control creates a barrier to new housing being available. Critics of rent control recommend that it be done away with—so that the poor and homeless no longer pay the price for middle-class renters' enjoyment of the benefits of rent control. They believe that an unregulated housing market operating by the law of supply and demand would meet the need for low-rent housing and therefore ease homelessness. "There is no other way," they insist, that "the crisis of homelessness can be solved."[17]

SQUATTERS HAVE NO RIGHTS

Much anger is aroused by the government's waffling on the issue of squatters in abandoned buildings. These buildings are technically owned by various local governments, which have taken them over from landlords for nonpayment of taxes. However, when squatters have moved into the buildings and repaired and improved them, some courts have decided that this can constitute ownership, or at least partial ownership.

Legally, it is a very murky area with conflicting opinions by different courts, with some courts reversing themselves and then reversing themselves yet again. To critics of government, however, the issue is clear-cut. Municipal "housing policy . . . lacks the character of law and has thus steadily eroded property rights in housing."[18] American law is grounded in property rights, they point out. If the city now holds a property because it has been seized for taxes, it owns it. Squatters who claim a right to the property for whatever reason are no more than thieves who have stolen it.

We may be sorry for those with holes in their shoes, critics state, but we do not give them the right to break into a shoe store and steal shoes. We may be sorry for those who are hungry, but we don't allow them to force entry into a supermarket in order to pilfer from the shelves. Why then should we allow the homeless to invade a locked building that they neither own nor rent and set up housekeeping there? Even if they make themselves comfortable by making repairs on the building, by what logic does this give them any rights of ownership?

— 92

Although squatters typically make improvements to abandoned buildings in order to live there, the conditions are still usually quite poor. This young man was squatting in a building in Philadelphia, Pennsylvania, in 1987.

Those who oppose squatters point out that it is often the poorest landlords who are victimized by them. One case is that of eighty-five-year-old Elzie Robinson, who, while working as a janitor, saved his money and bought four buildings in Harlem. When one had a fire, he shut it down until he could repair it. Squatters moved in, and he couldn't get them out.

One of the squatters—who, of course, paid no rent—brought charges against Mr. Robinson for not providing basic services like water, heat, and electricity. New York City Housing Court Judge Louis Friedman said the charges were justified. Mr. Robinson could begin eviction procedures, but as long as they lived in his building, he must provide heat, plumbing, and electricity. He had failed to do that, and so Mr. Robinson went to jail.

Another argument against squatters is that they are not the truly destitute homeless, but rather middle-class dropouts who voluntarily choose a lifestyle that allows them to sponge off society. Peter Weber investigated squatters on New York's Lower East Side for the *National Review*. He found a mix of punk rockers and skinheads, addicts and dope dealers, people who left their squats each morning dressed in business suits and bound for jobs, and antilandlord, antigovernment, anticapitalism leftists. "For the most part," he reported, "they were kids, college-age, white, articulate . . . rushing off to lectures at NYU or to eat the food churches give out for the truly poor."[19] He didn't find those who might be termed the *truly* homeless.

WELFARE FURTHERS HOMELESSNESS

If some critics of government intervention despair of government coddling squatters while the truly needy are neglected, others believe that "benign neglect," as Senator Daniel Patrick Moynahan once put it, is the best medicine for the large percentage of African Americans who are part of the homeless population. "Welfare has made invalids out of us," insists African American Bishop Luke Edwards. "Nobody owes us anything. Not the government, nobody." He views these programs as just "another form of slavery."[20]

Elizabeth Wright, editor of *Issues & Views*, which takes a conservative view of topics affecting African Americans, believes that "black energy was diverted away from the drive for economic independence" and concentrated instead on seeking social justice. She quotes Booker T. Washington to the effect that "no race that has anything to contribute to the markets of the world is long in any degree ostracized."[21] She believes that this is the legacy that black people sacrifice when they look to whites to provide such necessities as shelter.

Those of all races who criticize government programs for the homeless regard those on the receiving end as victims of the handouts. Critics are not without sympathy, but they refuse to sacrifice other values to it. They view homelessness as part of a deeper problem that has resulted in an underclass of poor people in the United States. And they agree with Myron Magnet of *Fortune* that this underclass's "dependence, its inability from one generation to another to participate in the larger society, the stunted development of its human potentialities— all this was fostered by the welfare system."[22]

8

THE IMPACT OF WELFARE REFORM

"Today we are ending welfare as we know it. But I hope this day will be remembered not for what it ended, but for what it began: a new day that offers hope, honors responsibility, rewards work and changes the terms of the debate so that no one in America ever feels again the need to criticize people who are poor or on welfare."

President Bill Clinton, upon signing
The Personal Responsibility and Work
Opportunity Reconciliation Act of 1996
(known as the Welfare Reform Act)[1]

Not all of those affected by the Welfare Reform Act are homeless, but all homeless people are affected by it. Their benefits, their status, their expectations, and their chances have been altered. Whether for better or worse is the latest debate between those who advocate government-financed aid programs and those who favor individual responsibility—known as the "bootstrap approach"—when dealing with the problems of homelessness.

The bootstrap, or tough-love, approach clearly influenced the shaping of the Welfare Reform Act. The philosophy of workfare—the shifting of those on welfare into job-training programs or municipal work programs—is spelled out in many provisions of the new law. The head of every family on welfare (including homeless single mothers) must have a job within two years or lose benefits. Other homeless adults lose their welfare benefits after just two months unless they find work or perform community service. No homeless persons of any age, whether they are working or not and regardless of need, can receive welfare benefits for longer than five years. Ending dependency is a major aim of the Welfare Reform Act.

Sometimes it works. "I thought it was going to be hard, but it wasn't," reports Felicia Fields of Greenville, Mississippi.[2] Ms. Fields had received $96 a month in cash and $213 in food stamps while on welfare. Now, as a receptionist for an insurance agency, a job she landed after the new rules forced her into a job-search class, she is proud to earn $825 a month.

Sometimes workfare doesn't work. In New York City Gloria Jimenez, fifty-one years old and crippled by arthritis in her hands, was enrolled in a workfare program and ordered to sweep the streets. When she missed a day because of the pain in her hands, she lost her welfare benefits. "I had worked all my life, and then I was forced to work at something I couldn't do,"[3] Ms. Jimenez lamented.

BLOCK GRANTS

The Welfare Reform Act reflects the view that homelessness is best dealt with at the local level rather than by catchall federal programs unsuited to different community conditions. Block grants—lump sums of money from the federal government—now go to states to spend on workfare, welfare, and homelessness as they see fit. Fourteen months after the act was passed, however, there was still a great deal of confusion among state and local governments as to how to administer its various provisions to help the homeless and other poor people.

One aim of the act was to cut the federal government's welfare costs. This was in keeping with efforts to balance the budget by cutting back on spending in all departments. Block grants to the states meant that the federal government no longer had to administer a vast assortment of welfare programs. The result has been across-the-board savings. However, the human cost of these savings, particularly to the homeless, has not yet been measured.

The new law did away with Aid to Dependent Families with Children (AFDC), a New Deal program of the 1930s designed to combat poverty, hunger, and homelessness during the Depression. Before it was ended in August 1996, AFDC had been providing "monthly cash benefits to 12.8 million people including more than 8 million children."[4] It was the main source of help for homeless children, most of whom are members of single-parent families.

The Welfare Reform Act also cut spending on food stamps by $24 billion over six years. The act gave states the right to set their own standards and payment levels for those who receive food stamps. In some states this meant further hardship for homeless recipients.

Most people support changes in the present welfare system, but know that cutting programs that benefit children, such as AFDC, can be risky. How can the cycle of homelessness be stopped if children are not provided with the food and shelter they need to focus on learning, and then working?

Federal funding for the Education for Homeless Children and Youth (EHCY) program was also cut by 20 percent in 1996. A survey of state coordinators for the EHCY covering forty states revealed that forty-one local education programs were eliminated as a result of the cuts. Some 15,690 homeless children were left without educational services.

Both legal and illegal immigrants among the homeless were hard hit by some of the cuts. Under the Welfare Reform Act, both those who had entered the country illegally and legal immigrants who had not become citizens were denied welfare benefits, social services, and food stamps. Nursing homes for the elderly began checking admission applications in order to exclude immigrants who are ineligible for Medicaid under the new law. Many of those who were denied had no place else to go.

In keeping with the belief that the private sector, not government, should deal with poverty and homelessness voluntarily, Hungarian-born financier George Soros pledged $50 million to help shield legal immigrants from homelessness. Meanwhile, legislators have become aware of public disapproval of some of the new law's harsh effects. It seems likely that some, but not all, of the aid programs will be restored to legal immigrants. This will come too late for Jose Santos Fuentes, a homeless day laborer from El Salvador, who froze to death in the ditch where he had been sleeping just outside the wealthy community of Glen Cove, New York.

WORKFARE: "IT BEATS BEGGING!"

Harsh as homelessness can be, not all of the homeless view the requirements of the Welfare Reform Act and the state and local programs stemming from it as placing a hardship on them. Some see it as a window of opportunity. "It beats begging,"[5] says Bayard, a homeless man who is a shelter regular and has been enrolled in a New York City program that employs homeless men to help clean the streets and parks.

That is the point, say champions of welfare reform. The homeless pay for the help they get with loss of self-esteem. Work restores self-esteem. Even jobs that are considered undesirable can be effective in this respect. Opal Caples, a divorced single mother with three children, is an example of both the benefits and limitations of welfare reform. When her ex-husband provided neither alimony nor child support, she escaped homelessness by leaving Chicago for Milwaukee to live with her sister. In Milwaukee, her welfare benefits were 50 percent more than she had been receiving in Chicago. (Before the Welfare Reform Act, Milwaukee taxpayers complained that more generous benefits drew homeless people to their city from the Chicago ghettos.)

"I liked that welfare check," Opal Caples remembers. She admits to having been one of those women "who don't want to work."[6] In 1996, however, when the administration of welfare shifted from the federal government to the states, she was forced to seek employment.

She got a job in a hospital, working nights. She scrubbed floors, disposed of waste matter, and cleaned toilets and urinals. Despite the nature of the work, she really didn't mind it too much. "I think it's different for me now,"[7] she said.

However, the score isn't really in yet on Opal Caples. She has had attendance problems with her job. She has problems finding someone to look after her three children while she is at work. If she lost her job, Opal Caples and her children could not get welfare. There would be some public assistance for the children, but under Wisconsin rules, not working would deprive Opal Caples of welfare. If for some reason she and her children could no longer stay with her sister, they could end up homeless.

WISCONSIN WORKS

The case of Opal Caples and her children was just one of many handled by Wisconsin Works, a Milwaukee program that divided the city into six districts and enlisted private agencies to handle its 25,000 cases of homelessness and poverty. Known as privatization—the hiring of both for-profit and non-profit organizations to take over government functions—the Milwaukee experiment has attracted national attention. The program actually began in 1993, but it wasn't until 1996 that the Welfare Reform Act provided both the block-grant funds and the legal backing to enforce the Wisconsin Works philosophy.

William Martin, in charge of Wisconsin Works, explains that philosophy. "We start from a moral premise," he says, "that it is simply unconscionable to leave somebody on welfare. If the goal is to get somebody out of poverty, the only way to do it is to get them a job that pays better [than welfare]."[8]

The program classifies those it helps—the homeless, people who were on welfare, others in poverty—in four groupings. The first, the "job-ready," receive leads for jobs, coaching for interviews, and vouchers for child care, but no money.[9] The next group are steered into jobs with private employers who receive some part of the employee's salary from the state and city government. People in the third group are given workfare jobs performing community services like picking up litter or shoveling snow. The last group, those suffering from addictions or mental illness, must go into therapy or drug and alcohol addiction programs for twenty-eight hours a week. They receive $518 a month, and their progress is strictly monitored in order to place them in community service programs or other jobs as soon as possible.

Milwaukee and the state of Wisconsin are committed to making workfare successful. Top officials view it as the long-term solution to homelessness. They've been helped by an unexpected increase in the block grant that states receive from the federal government under the Welfare Reform Law.

The law based the amount of the block grants on the number of people receiving welfare in 1993–1994. But that number dropped 26 percent nationwide by 1997. As a result, the federal government distributed a bonus payment of $2.6 billion to the states.

Wisconsin has been spending all of its share of the extra money on programs like Milwaukee's Wisconsin Works. The annual amount the state spends per needy family has been raised from $9,700 in 1996 to $15,700 in 1997. Other states have also used the money constructively. The state of Michigan is investing the bonus in hiring additional social workers. Illinois is spending it on child-care programs.

THE NEW YORK STORY

Not all the states, however, are using all the money to help the poor and the homeless. Some are using it for highway building programs, to finance tax cuts, or to build sports stadiums or other municipal projects. In some states fierce legislative battles have been waged over how to spend the extra money. In Texas, California, and New York, where nearly one third of those on welfare live, there have been ongoing struggles among legislators over spending under the provisions of the Welfare Reform Act.

New York City avoids state legislators' wrangling by acting on its own. With the largest population of homeless people of any city in the country, New York City began a tough-love style of reform with the installation of Republican Rudolph Giuliani as mayor in 1993. At that time there were 1.1 million people on the municipal welfare rolls. Over the next four years Giuliani's hard-line approach reduced that number by 320,000.

By the end of 1997, New York City had put in place the nation's largest workfare program. Some 200,000 poor and homeless people have been put to work performing community service-oriented tasks that enhance the quality of life for all people in the five boroughs of the city. A reward-and-punishment approach is used to accomplish this, with some homeless shelters denying beds to adults who refuse to do community service jobs in exchange for them.

Supporters of Mayor Giuliani's programs say that they have greatly eased the problems of homelessness. There are nowhere near the number of homeless beggars on the streets and in the subways as there were when he came to office. There are still homeless people sleeping in doorways and on grates, but their numbers have been greatly reduced by police actions to move them along. As a result, the homeless in New York City are much less visible than they used to be. While statistics show that they were rarely dangerous, the often dirty and ragged street people had seemed menacing to much of the public. Now New Yorkers don't feel as threatened by the homeless as they once did.

A side effect of their reduced presence is that New York City no longer seems quite as dangerous to tourists. The hotel, restaurant, and entertainment businesses, as well as other enterprises dependent on tourism, have profited by this. The economy of New York City has grown accordingly.

"It is an enormous change," is how Fred Siegel of the Progressive Policy Institute measures the Giuliani reforms. During the previous city administration, he points out, "there was no attempt to come to grips with the cost of dependency to the city, and the cost of dependency to the people caught in it."[10]

Not all those concerned about homelessness are happy about expanding these reforms. Nor do they view them as successful. City planner Susan Friedland, for instance, believes that "the Mayor's policy on welfare reform is cruel and inhumane."[11]

Others point to reports in *The New York Times* that "dozens of homeless families still sleep on the floors of government offices each night, and thousands more have been turned away."[12] City statistics reveal that while only three families were refused emergency shelter in 1994, in the first ten months of

1997 there were 7,747 families turned away. During 1996 and 1997, there was a 15 percent increase in the number of homeless people seeking beds in city shelters. That works out to an average of 7,119 every night. This reversed a trend in which the number had been falling.

Likewise, the number of New York City children in foster care has grown by 40 percent since 1995. Many of these children were taken from parents who could not provide adequate shelter for them. Many of them were mistreated in the foster homes in which they were placed. Caseworkers assigned to monitor the mistreated children found that 43 percent of them were abused a second time. So many of them were then taken out of their foster homes that the city was unable to find adequate housing for them. Many children were forced to sleep on makeshift beds in city offices.

FOR BETTER OR WORSE?

Advocates for the homeless fear that the situation will only get worse. By the end of 1998, almost 180,000 adults in New York State will lose their welfare benefits altogether. The same is true for many of the homeless throughout the country.

The question is whether city and state governments have the ability, the money, and the will to pick up the slack. Will local programs financed by block grants really succeed in "ending welfare as we know it,"[13] as President Clinton promised? Is there a safety net to provide food, clothing, and shelter for the least fortunate of America's people? Or is there only a Welfare Reform Act gap where the safety net used to be?

According to the experts, a yes answer of sorts is possible to those questions. They say that "the safety net is growing in some places and growing holes in others."[14] The problems of homelessness will be eased or aggravated accordingly.

AFTERWORD

Even as we pass laws and institute programs to deal with homelessness, hard questions remain unanswered. For instance, are there really enough jobs available in the United States to put the homeless to work? Even if there are, financial experts tell us that if the unemployment rate drops below 5 percent, inflation will result, prices will rise, and the economy—which means all of us—will suffer.

Some cities, New York among them, have laid off employees and replaced them with homeless people forced to take over these tasks in exchange for shelter. Municipal workers' unions have protested. They have set about organizing the homeless to demand the replacement of the food and shelter vouchers and small amounts of money they receive with a living wage.

This, in turn, has city and state governments protesting that if they have to pay the homeless the minimum wage for workfare, they won't be able to afford such programs. If they don't, say advocates for the homeless, the workers will be little more than slave labor. But if the minimum wage is paid, the cuts in other city programs will result in reduction of vital services such as school maintenance, garbage collection, and public transportation for those whose taxes support the city.

THE IMMIGRANT HOMELESS

Another unresolved problem involves immigration. Do people have the right to come to the United States from another country and receive some form of government assistance if they become homeless? Or should these homeless immigrants and their children be left in the streets to fend for themselves? Some city governments refuse to deny benefits to homeless immigrants. Nor do they take steps to determine their legal status. Critics claim that this results in more and more illegal immigrants being drawn to these communities.

They say that this puts a strain on the local economy and ultimately on the taxpayers. They question whether taxpayers are obligated to support homeless people who have entered this country illegally. Others take the position that we are a nation of immigrants with a duty to help today's newcomers, regardless of their status.

MORALITY: A HIDDEN AGENDA?

Questions of morality also remain unanswered. Births to unmarried teenage mothers have created a pattern of homelessness being passed on from one generation to the next. In an attempt to deal with this, the Welfare Reform Act allocates $400 million to teach abstinence from sexual intercourse, but the Act provides no money for other forms of birth control.

Also, the federal government will pay $20 million every year to each of the five states that shows the greatest reduction in births to unwed mothers. Champions of the homeless view such funding as an invasion of people's right to privacy and personal choice. Both civil-liberties activists and conservatives are leery of such government intrusion.

The intrusion pushes over into another area, that of forcing unwed fathers to pay child support. The Welfare Reform Act requires homeless women to provide information about the fathers of their children. If they do not, they will lose 25 percent of their benefits. The idea is that the federal government will then use a national database to locate the fathers and force them to pay.

Opponents point out that some women may be pushed into admissions of having had sex with more than one man to show that they don't know who the father is. Others may name an innocent man. Some feminist groups and some groups on the religious right, who believe that it is imperative to make men responsible for the children they have fathered, answer objections by pointing out that genetic testing can establish fatherhood in contested cases.

How Much Sacrifice?

Other thorny issues are still being debated. Should the homeless who are mentally ill be housed in group homes or returned to institutions? Should homeless addicts be denied shelter if they continue to use drugs or alcohol? With no Medicaid and no health insurance, how can treatment be assured for the homeless who are ill?

Should small low-income housing units be distributed among stable neighborhoods, or will this just spread problems like drugs, crime, disease, and others? If low-income housing for the homeless is built in specific areas set aside for it, will the result be the ghettos of tomorrow? Just how much in the way of support services should the formerly homeless receive after they are housed? How much help are they entitled to, and how much is just making them more dependent?

When we ask these questions, and when we introduce the opposing views, we are too often presenting the more extreme positions in evaluating the homelessness problem. In fact, both advocates for the homeless and the critics of the programs designed to help them are often sensitive to each other's positions, open to new ideas, flexible in their approach to problems and solutions, and willing to compromise. The majority recognize that there must be a balance between the needs of the homeless and the needs of society as a whole.

The 1993–1994 Interagency Council's *Federal Plan to Break the Cycle of Homelessness* set as its goal "a decent home and a suitable living environment"[1] for all Americans. But just how much are ordinary citizens willing to sacrifice to attain that goal? That may be the biggest question of all.

NOTES

Chapter One

1. Ralph da Costa Nunez, *The New Poverty: Homeless Families in America* (New York: Insight Books, 1996), p. 171.

2. U. S. Department of Housing and Urban Development, *Priority: Home! The Federal Plan to Break the Cycle of Homelessness* (Washington, DC: U. S. Government Printing Office, 1994), p. 21.

3. Bruce Link, "Life-time and Five-Year Prevalence of Homelessness in the United States" in *American Journal of Public Health*, December, 1994. (Taken from National Coalition for the Homeless Fact Sheet #2, p. 3).

4. Bureau of the Census, *Fact Sheet for 1990 Decennial Census Counts of Persons in Selected Locations Where Homeless Persons Are Found* (Washington, DC: Bureau of the Census, Population Division, CPH-L-87, 1997), p. 2.

5. Joel Blau, *The Visible Poor: Homelessness in the United States* (New York: Oxford University Press, 1992), p. 47.

6. Jonathan Kozol, *Amazing Grace: The Lives of Children and the Conscience of a Nation* (New York: Crown Publishers, 1995), p. 21.

CHAPTER TWO

1. Howard Zinn, *A People's History of the United States* (New York: Harper & Row, 1980), p. 43.

2. Zinn, p. 49.

3. Peter H. Rossi, *Down and Out in America: The Origins of Homelessness* (Chicago: The University of Chicago Press, 1989), p. 17.

4. Richard B. Morris, *The Forging of the Union: 1781–1789* (New York: Harper & Row, 1987), p. 178.

5. Morris, p. 179.

6. Roy Rosenzweig and Elizabeth Blackmar, *The Park and the People: A History of Central Park* (Ithaca, NY: Cornell University Press, 1992), p. 64.

7. Andrea Warren, *Orphan Train Rider: One Boy's True Story* (Boston: Houghton Mifflin, 1996), p.17.

8. Joel Blau, *The Visible Poor: Homelessness in the United States* (New York: Oxford University Press, 1992), p. 34.

9. Blau, p. 34.

10. Rossi, p. 19.

11. Michael B. Katz, *In the Shadow of the Poorhouse: A Social History of Welfare in America* (New York: Basic Books, 1986), p. 88.

12. *Chronicle of the 20th Century* (Mount Kisco, NY: Chronicle Publications, 1987), p. 116.

13. Katz, p. 207.

14. Zinn, pp. 379–380.

15. Ted Gottfried, *Eleanor Roosevelt: First Lady of the 20th Century* (Danbury, CT: Franklin Watts, 1997), p. 76.

16. Alice S. Baum and Donald W. Burnes, *A Nation in Denial: The Truth About Homelessness* (San Francisco: Westview Press, 1993), p. 104.

Chapter Three

1. Jonathan Kozol, *Amazing Grace: The Lives of Children and the Conscience of a Nation* (New York: Crown Publishers, 1995), p. 45.

2. Ralph da Costa Nunez, *The New Poverty: Homeless Families in America* (New York: Insight Books, 1996), pp. 70–71.

3. Joel Blau, *The Visible Poor: Homelessness in the United States* (New York: Oxford University Press, 1992), p. 18.

4. U. S. Department of Housing and Urban Development, *Priority: Home! The Federal Plan to Break the Cycle of Homelessness* (Washington, DC: U. S. Government Printing Office, 1994), p. 11.

5. HUD, *Priority: Home!*, p. 23.

6. *Encyclopedia & Dictionary of Medicine, Nursing and Allied Health: Fifth Edition* (Philadelphia: Harcourt Brace Jovanovich, 1992), pp. 1196–1197.

7. HUD, *Priority: Home!*, p. 24.

8. National Coalition for the Homeless Fact Sheet # 1, p. 1.

9. *The African American Market* (New York: Packaged Facts, 1995), p. 39.

10. HUD, *Priority: Home!*, p. 24.

11. National Coalition for the Homeless Fact Sheet # 5, p. 1.

12. HUD, *Priority: Home!*, p. 33.

13. National Coalition for the Homeless Fact Sheet # 6, p. 1.

14. HUD, *Priority: Home!*, p. 24.

15. Ruth Sidel, *Keeping Women and Children Last: America's War on the Poor* (New York: Penguin Books, 1996), p. 173.

16. *The State of America's Children: Yearbook*, 1997 (Washington: Children's Defense Fund, 1997), p. 7.

17. Allison Mitchell, "Clinton Faces Off With Congress on Trade," in *The New York Times*, September 17, 1997.

CHAPTER FOUR

1. Lisa Orr, Ed., *The Homeless: Opposing Viewpoints* (San Diego: Greenhaven Press, 1990), p.13.

2. Katie de Koster, Ed., *Poverty: Opposing Viewpoints* (San Diego: Greenhaven Press), 1994, p. 65.

3. Linda Wheeler, "Parents of 14 Accused of Misusing Public Funds," *Washington Post*, March 12, 1990.

4. Alice S. Baum and Donald W. Burnes, *A Nation in Denial: The Truth About Homelessness* (San Francisco: Westview Press, 1993), p. 137.

5. James D. Wright and Eleanor Weber, *Homelessness and Health* (Washington, DC: McGraw-Hill, 1987), p. 9.

6. Baum and Burnes, p. 141.

7. Baum and Burnes, p. 142.

8. Baum and Burnes, p. 148.

9. de Koster, p. 65.

10. de Koster, p. 65.

11. de Koster, pp. 65–66.

12. de Koster, p. 71.

13. de Koster, p. 67.

14. John Leo, "Homeless Rights, Community Wrongs," *U. S. News & World Report*, July 24, 1989, p. 56.

15. Orr, p.48.

16. de Koster, p. 71.

17. Sol Stern, "A Fix for Homelessness: Going to Work," *New York Post*, August 19, 1997.

CHAPTER FIVE

1. Jonathan Kozol, *Amazing Grace: The Lives of Children and the Conscience of a Nation* (New York: Crown Publishers, 1995), p. 78.

2. National Coalition for the Homeless Fact Sheet # 1, p. 4.

3. Ibid.

4. Randy Kennedy, "Many Tenants Are Struggling To Pay Rent," *The New York Times*, September 8, 1997.

5. Kennedy.

6. *The State of America's Children: Yearbook*, 1997 (Washington,DC: Children's Defense Fund, 1997), p. 14.

7. Margaret O. Hyde, *The Homeless: Profiling the Problem* (Hillside, NJ: Enslow Publishers, 1989), pp. 59–60.

8. Kennedy.

9. U. S. Department of Housing and Urban Development, *Priority: Home! The Federal Plan to Break the Cycle of Homelessness* (Washington, DC: U. S. Government Printing Office, 1994), p. 33.

10. Kozol, p. 52.

11. Lisa Orr, Ed., *The Homeless: Opposing Viewpoints* (San Diego: Greenhaven Press, 1990), p.113.

CHAPTER SIX

1. Ralph da Costa Nunez, *The New Poverty: Homeless Families in America* (New York: Insight Books, 1996), p. 15.

2. Ruth Sidel, *Keeping Women and Children Last: America's War on the Poor* (New York: Penguin Books, 1996), p. 166. [Quoting President Franklin D. Roosevelt's annual message to Congress, 1944.]

3. National Coalition for the Homeless 1997 flyer.

4. U. S. Department of Housing and Urban Development, *Priority: Home! The Federal Plan to Break the Cycle of Homelessness* (Washington, DC: U. S. Government Printing Office, 1994), p. 87.

5. Randy Kennedy, "Many Tenants Are Struggling to Pay Rent," *The New York Times*, September 9, 1997.

6. Kennedy.

7. Author's interview with Lee Kreiling, former director of Scattered Site Housing for the New York City Coalition of the Homeless, October 9, 1997.

8. Nunez, p. 195.

9. HUD, *Priority: Home!*, p. 25.

CHAPTER SEVEN

1. Katie de Koster, Ed., *Poverty: Opposing Viewpoints* (San Diego: Greenhaven Press, 1994), p. 224.

2. Lisa Orr, Ed., *The Homeless: Opposing Viewpoints* (San Diego: Greenhaven Press, 1990), p. 115.

3. Orr, p. 115.

4. Orr, p. 101.

5. Orr, p. 101.

6. Jack Kemp, "An Inquiry into the Nature and Causes of Poverty in America and How to Combat It," from a speech at the Heritage Foundation, June 6, 1990.

7. de Koster, p. 216.

8. Jason DeParle, "Welfare Law Weighs Heavy in Delta, Where Jobs Are Few," *The New York Times*, October 16, 1997.

9. DeParle.

10. DeParle.

11. DeParle.

12. Ernest van den Haag, "Who Goes Homeless," *National Review*, March 1, 1993.

13. van den Haag.

14. Orr, p. 159.

15. Orr, p. 160.

16. Orr, p. 163.

17. Orr, p. 167.

18. Orr, p. 187.

19. Peter Weber, "Scenes From the Squatting Life," *National Review*, February 27, 1987, p. 29.

20. de Koster, p. 153.

21. Elizabeth Wright, "Legacy Lost: The Road Not Taken," *Issues and Views*, Spring, 1992, p. 1.

22. Myron Magnet, "The Homeless," *Fortune*, November 23, 1987, p. 170.

CHAPTER EIGHT

1. Francis X. Clines, "Clinton Signs Bill Cutting Welfare; States in New Role," *The New York Times*, August 23, 1996.

2. Jason DeParle, "Welfare Law Weighs Heavy in Delta, Where Jobs Are Few," *The New York Times*, October 16, 1997.

3. Joe Sexton, "Privacy and Pride Are Submerged at Busy Workfare Evaluation Site," *The New York Times*, October 13, 1997.

4. Clines.

5. Author's interview, with Bayard, a homeless man, New York City, October 29, 1997.

6. Jason DeParle, "Getting Opal Caples To Work," *The New York Times Magazine*, August 24, 1997, p. 37.

7. DeParle, "Caples," p. 60.

8. DeParle, "Caples," p. 36.

9. DeParle, "Caples," p. 35.

10. Rachel L. Swarns, "320,000 Have Left Welfare, But Where Do They Go From Here?," *The New York Times*, October 29, 1997.

11. Felicia R. Lee, "Park Slope's Proud Democrats Feel Tug of Strained Loyalties," *The New York Times*, November 1, 1997.

12. Swarns.

13. Clines.

14. DeParle, "Caples," p. 59.

AFTERWORD
1. U. S. Department of Housing and Urban Development, *Priority: Home! The Federal Plan to Break the Cycle of Homelessness* (Washington, DC: U. S. Government Printing Office, 1994), p. 67.

FURTHER READING

Baum, Alice S., and Donald W. Burnes. *A Nation in Denial: The Truth About Homelessness.* San Francisco: Westview Press, 1993.

Bode, Janet. *Beating the Odds: Stories of Unexpected Achievers.* New York: Franklin Watts, 1991.

Bode, Janet, and Stan Mack. *Heartbreak and Roses: Real Life Stories of Troubled Love.* New York: Delacorte Press, 1994 (paperback 1996).

De Koster, Katie, Ed., *Poverty: Opposing Viewpoints.* San Diego: Greenhaven Press, 1994.

Hyde, Margaret O. *The Homeless: Profiling the Problem.* Hillside, NJ: Enslow Publishers, 1989.

Kozol, Jonathan. *Amazing Grace: The Lives of Children and the Conscience of a Nation.* New York: Crown Publishers, 1995.

Kozol, Jonathan. *Savage Inequalities: Children in America's Schools.* New York: Crown Publishers, 1991.

Nunez, Ralph da Costa. *The New Poverty: Homeless Families in America.* New York: Insight Books, 1996.

Sidel, Ruth. *Keeping Women and Children Last: America's War on the Poor.* New York: Penguin Books, 1996.

Warren, Andrea. *Orphan Train Rider: One Boy's True Story.* Boston: Houghton Mifflin Company, 1996.

ORGANIZATIONS
TO CONTACT

Bureau of the Census
Population Division
Washington, DC 20233-8800
(301) 457-2378

The Commonwealth Fund
1 East 75th Street
New York, NY 10021-2692
(888) 777-2744

Doe Fund
232 East 84th Street
New York, NY 10028
(212) 628-5207

Heritage Foundation
214 Massachusetts Avenue NE
Washington, DC 20002
(202) 546-4400

Interagency Council on the Homeless
451 Seventh Street, Suite 7274
Washington, DC 20410-0000
(202) 708-1480

Manhattan Institute
52 Vanderbilt Avenue
New York, NY 10017
(212) 599-7000

National Coalition for the Homeless
1612 K Street NW, #1004
Washington, DC 20006-2802
(202) 775-1316

National Low Income Housing Coalition
1012 14th Street NW, #1200
Washington, DC 20005-3410
(202) 662-1530

National Resource Center on
    Homelessness and Mental Illness
262 Delaware Avenue
Delmar, NY 12054
(800) 444-7515

The Urban Institute
2100 M Street NW
Washington, DC 20037
(202) 833-7200

U. S. Department of Agriculture
Rural Housing Service
Rural Economic and Community Development
14th Street and Independence Avenue SW
Washington, DC 20250-1533
(202) 690-1533

INDEX